## Praise for *The Spirit of Harriet Tubman*

IIIIIIIIIIIIIIIIIIIIIIIIIIIIIIIIIIIIIIIIIIIIIIIIIIIIIIIIIIIIIIIIIIIIIIIIIIIIIIIIIIIIIIIIII

*"Wow! An extraordinary and inspiring story,
one of power and heart. Read this and Harriet
will touch your spirit and change you for the good."*

— Jack Kornfield, author of *A Path with Heart*

♦

*"A powerful and astonishing book on the
liberator Harriet Tubman, whose courage and vision,
determination, and love will light the underground of our
lives. Spring Washam brings to us her life and Harriet's
in a voice that is both beautiful and courageous."*

Roshi Joan Halifax, Abbot, Upaya Zen Center

♦

*"Mother Harriet, as an awakened bodhisattva,
knows that real freedom is realizing the essence of
everything, and to do that, our abolition practice must also
be a spiritual practice where we are allying with the unseen
world of beings who are working alongside us to get us and
everything free. . . . In this text Spring has consented to allow
Mother Harriet to speak through her to offer to the world a
vital message of hope as well as a call to action."*

— from the foreword by Lama Rod Owens

❖

## Praise for *A Fierce Heart*

||||||||||||||||||||||||||||||||||||||||||||||||||||||

*"Washam brings considerable gifts for conveying
her vision of personal change and offers vivid, inspiring
testimony to the power of Buddhism (and other
wisdom traditions) to help heal suffering."*

— *Publishers Weekly*

❖

The Spirit of

# HARRIET
# TUBMAN

# ALSO BY SPRING WASHAM

*A Fierce Heart:*
*Finding Strength, Courage,*
*and Wisdom in Any Moment*

The above is available at
your local bookstore,
or may be ordered by visiting:

Hay House USA: www.hayhouse.com®
Hay House Australia: www.hayhouse.com.au
Hay House UK: www.hayhouse.co.uk
Hay House India: www.hayhouse.co.in

The Spirit of

# HARRIET TUBMAN

*Awakening from
the Underground*

## SPRING WASHAM

**HAY HOUSE, INC.**
Carlsbad, California • New York City
London • Sydney • New Delhi

*Published in the United States by:* Hay House, Inc.: www.hayhouse.com®
*Published in Australia by:* Hay House Australia Pty. Ltd.: www.hayhouse.com.au
*Published in the United Kingdom by:* Hay House UK, Ltd.: www.hayhouse.co.uk
*Published in India by:* Hay House Publishers India: www.hayhouse.co.in

*Interior design:* Bryn Starr Best
*Cover illustration:* Lobsang Melendez Ahuanari
*Cover design:* Claudine Mansour

Lines from "The Hill We Climb" copyright © 2021 by Amanda Gorman. Used by permission of the author.

Photo of Harriet Tubman on page 146 reproduced courtesy of the Ohio History Connection, image AL03231.

**Cataloging-in-Publication Data is on file
at the Library of Congress**

Hardcover ISBN: 978-1-4019-6322-4
E-book ISBN: 978-1-4019-6323-1
Audiobook ISBN: 978-1-4019-6324-8

10  9  8  7  6  5  4  3  2  1
1st edition, January 2023

Printed in the United States of America

SUSTAINABLE FORESTRY INITIATIVE
Certified Chain of Custody
Promoting Sustainable Forestry
www.sfiprogram.org
SFI-01268
SFI label applies to the text stock

*This book is dedicated to all the
abolitionists, freedom fighters, and supporters of
the Underground Railroad. It's also dedicated
to Dr. Martin Luther King Jr., one of the
greatest conductors in the universe.*

# CONTENTS

# FOREWORD

iiiiiiiiiiiiiiiiiiiiiiiiiiiiiiiiiiiiiiiiiiiiiiiiiiiiiiii

◆

*We are soldiers in the army.*
*We have to fight although we have to cry.*
*We've got to hold up the blood-stained banner.*
*We've got to hold it up until we die!*

— "WE ARE SOLDIERS,"
TRADITIONAL BLACK GOSPEL HYMN

❖

During the summer of the 2020 quarantine, Spring and I chatted one afternoon about her connection to Mother Harriet Tubman, a connection that had resulted first in an online gathering space called the Church of Harriet and later developed into the inspiration for this very text. Spring spoke of the intensity of opening to the immensity of Mother Harriet's awakened consciousness, a series of experiences that would often leave her deeply inspired but also incredibly depleted and shaken. Mother Harriet was asking her to write a book to clarify aspects of her life that had been previously misunderstood. I empathized with Spring. I was not only serving the grief of the pandemic but also having to navigate a lot of powerful energies, so I too was feeling weary. I loved Mother Harriet and had a deep appreciation and reverence for what she did to free our people, but I remember thinking that I really couldn't handle what she was serving Spring!

Later that year, a student offered me a large framed portrait of Mother Harriet and a hoodie with her picture on the front. The portrait is the famous shot of her in her late elder years, sitting in a rocking chair draped in white. Her left hand is resting on the chair's arm and she gazes just past the camera. This student felt that Mother Harriet was attempting to connect to me as well. I was appreciative of the offering but still didn't feel at that time that I had a strong connection to her.

In the iconic photo, her face as well as her expression are hard to describe, even as I sit here gazing at the picture in my practice room. It's as if her face is carved of stone, but it doesn't feel rigid or hard. It feels like her face as well as her whole body has been shaped by the richness of the earth itself. She radiates the power of mountains, emanating an energy of foundation and unshakability, embracing the wisdom and fortitude of someone who had no choice but to force the world to bend to her will. Her eyes are clear and swirling with intense joy that has known the darkest sorrow. Her eyes are doing much more than gazing beyond the camera, they are gazing into the unseen heart of this world to which she came free of delusion. She is wrapped in love, held by stillness, and yet she is tired. She seems to be communicating, "I've done what I can, and I am grateful."

When I was offered the portrait, I rested it in my practice space on a chair because I felt she wanted a seat instead of being hung on the wall. I draped the frame in a white shawl and prepared a vase of various colorful flowers beside the frame. Soon the practice space as well as my whole house felt weighted, as if gravity had intensified or as if the air had thickened so every moment and breath took even more effort. I have often experienced being haunted, and even then I could shake off the spirits around me. But she was not a spirit. She was not haunting. She refused to be shaken off.

The picture on the hoodie was a younger image, perhaps from her days when she was active in the Underground Railroad. It was a nice hoodie, and as it was nearing fall, I wanted to start wearing it. However, each time I attempted to put it on, I felt an intense foreboding. It was another expression of the heaviness that had come over the house. I knew that this was significant, but I put it out of my mind.

Over the next few weeks, the heaviness in the house got more intense. By then I knew it was Mother Harriet trying to get my attention. I was scared, not of her spirit, but of what she might be trying to get me to do. I cannot fathom the level of courage and love that propelled her from enduring slavery into escaping, choosing to return at least 13 times to rescue our people, and later even deciding to enlist with the Union Army. It was too much. I was barely surviving the intensity of a deepening pandemic and the demands of the unseen world, and I really didn't need a new set of demands.

However, one afternoon it was too much. The weight of Mother Harriet's spirit became unbearable. So I went into my practice space, gazed at the portrait of Mother Harriet like an irritated child, and asked her what she wanted. The power of her spirit formed language in my mind as she responded as if amused, *"Not much. You can wear the hoodie, but if you wear it you are signing up for the Great Work in this life."*

"What work?"

*"Just the work of getting our people free. Like me, you must become a conductor on this path of freedom."*

As I received the last transmission, I felt an openness and joy bloom. It felt like Mother Harriet was simply reminding me of something that I had long ago committed to doing. I responded with "Of course, I'm on board."

The intense energy in the space lifted and it was replaced by lightness and a kind of sweetness. Mother Harriet had recruited me into the service of freedom work, and it felt good and right to be joining this work again. Even in this moment I can hear the old Black gospel hymn that goes, "We are soldiers in the army," and this army is a sacred army armed with love and guided by great generals like Mother Harriet.

When I shared this experience with Spring, she confirmed that Mother Harriet was indeed here to recruit folks for what Mother Harriet has called "The Spiritual Underground Railroad," or what I call *The Spirit Underground*. We are still not yet free. From the perspective of the traditional bodhisattva path or the path of Buddhist sainthood, we keep working until all beings are free. Through Spring, Mother Harriet has offered a profound insight into who and what she is.

Mother Harriet is an awakened bodhisattva who has emanated into this world many times to help free beings. In her last physical incarnation, she was Harriet Tubman, called Moses, who chose to come to disrupt the institution of slavery by showing us how to get free. It was love that directed her choice to be here with us in the body of a Black woman born into slavery, and it was the same love that guided her life so she could leave this world freer than she had found it. I call her Mother because she embodies the great cosmic feminine consciousness, which is an expression of space itself. She is the mother because freedom is never possible without remembering the inherent space we are being held in.

Now we find ourselves in the depths of an apocalypse, witnessing and experiencing a painful collapse of relationships, communities, and institutions. We are in trouble and our world system has sent out an SOS. Mother Harriet has returned, like so many other great awakened beings, not in a physical body, but within the consciousness realm, working to awaken the consciousness of anyone who is ready to listen. She, like many awakened beings, is returning because we are in the depths of crisis in this world system.

Later in her life, Mother Harriet became known as Moses, echoing the great liberator of the children of Israel out of Egypt in what we call the Exodus. Mother Harriet emanated here on purpose to free Black people embodying the power of Moses himself because Black people had been praying for Moses to free them as he freed his people. Awakened bodhisattvas go where they are needed and skillfully become what people need in order to help free them from suffering.

Mother Harriet, like all bodhisattvas, only wants us to be free because what we are experiencing is the epitome of suffering. When Mother Harriet speaks of freedom, she is saying that we all deserve to have access to all the recourse we need to experience wellness, safety, community belonging, and happiness. It is processing the agency to make choices or set boundaries about the care we need and how we wish those around us to relate to us. This level of freedom is tended to by our overall ethic of reducing harm to ourselves and others. Yet ultimately, freedom is realizing the very nature of our minds, which is the same nature of all phenomena. Mother Harriet is here to help us remember who we really are.

Mother Harriet was one of the leaders of the abolitionist movement. Her work, along with the tireless and dangerous work of many abolitionists, laid a practical foundation for the practice of abolition. Abolition was more than the work of ending slavery; it was and is first dreaming liberation and then working to awaken that dream in the world. However, one of the most important lessons Mother Harriet teaches us here is that her abolition and the abolition that is needed right now must be the union of both social and ultimate liberation. As we work to free people from harm in the relative world, we must also be working to experience liberation from all suffering by remembering the nature of our minds and the nature of all phenomena. Mother Harriet, as an awakened bodhisattva, knows that real freedom is realizing the essence of everything, and to do that our abolition practice must also be a spiritual practice where we are allying with the unseen world of beings who are working alongside us to get us and everything free. I can hear Mother Harriet saying now that if we ain't praying and asking for help from the beings in the unseen world, then we ain't serious about getting free.

Anyone who channels has experienced the challenge of opening our minds and bodies to other intelligent and sometimes awakened consciousnesses. You know what the impact of that engagement can be on our bodies and minds. In this text Spring has consented to allow Mother Harriet to speak through her to offer to the world a vital message of hope as well as a call to action. This offering has been a beautiful and difficult labor for Spring. I am grateful for this offering and for knowing through this text that Mother Harriet and countless other beings are in solidarity with us and our struggle in this very second.

This text has reminded me that we are in the depth of heart of spiritual warfare, and it is our work now to join this struggle against delusion, hate, and apathy. When you read this text, allow your mind, heart, and body to open to what Mother Harriet is offering us. This is the balm we need to soothe the violence of having forgotten who we are. I hope that you will be ready to join the sacred army and join us in the Spirit Underground for this Great Work, the work of liberation for all beings.

Lama Rod Owens

For my dear sister Spring

Writing and remembering on the ancestral lands of the Creek, Cherokee, and Muskogee People, land the forgetful ones call Atlanta, Georgia

# AUTHOR'S PREFACE

Within the vast space between heaven and earth, the spirit of Harriet Tubman is steadily awakening and rising again. Harriet Tubman now lives within the universe, yet her powerful gaze remains fixed and focused on us. Her timing is precise; we're on the brink of something transformational and a new generation is crying out for help.

To all the beautiful readers of this book, it is my deepest prayer that you will find true inspiration, hope, and profound courage within these pages. Writing this book has completely changed me. It has taken me on a holy, heartrending, mind-bending journey, and with every word, I've been pushed to grow and understand the world and my own life's path in an entirely new way. It's my greatest hope that it will do the same for you.

The idea of writing about Harriet Tubman arose quite unexpectedly. I'm not a historian, an academic, or a literary expert. I was, instead, guided by the spirit of Harriet Tubman herself to share with you the details of her spiritual journey, her fearless heart, and her compassionate guidance for the world today. At times the writing process was painfully distressing, and at other times exhilarating and magnificent. I discovered—actually, rediscovered—the vastness of the human heart and its capacity to hold *everything* in a compassionate embrace. I learned to trust my own heart's ability to accompany Harriet down roads that, not long ago, would have been too frightening to traverse. Through her I continue to find an embodied courage that allows our spirits to merge at the intersection of Love and Truth.

In this book, I attempt to weave together our unique voices. The first is Harriet Tubman's, including her stories, messages, teachings for today, and channeled conversations I've had with her. The second is my voice as your guide, occasional teacher, researcher, and diligent scribe who has documented every step of Harriet's and my incredible journey. And finally, me—my personal story, actual thoughts, day-to-day truths, and honest account as one of Harriet Tubman's students and passengers traveling with her on the spirit Underground Railroad.

I've tried my best to structure the narrative in a way that makes sense; however, we are often traveling very fast, so you may need to slow way down and reread some sections to let Harriet's profound presence in. She is asking something from all of us, to participate in a deeper process and enter into a sacred space where you can pray and undertake collective and personal healing along the way. That is the common thread throughout the book.

Over the years, there have been many inaccuracies written about Harriet Tubman. As historical documents surface, many of these are being cleared up. I am aware that a book like this may engender controversy and possibly cause more confusion, and if that happens, I deeply apologize. I believe that the benefits outweigh the risks.

So, here we are, the three of us—you, the reader; me, who communicated with the spirit of Harriet Tubman, who is in awe of it all, sharing my own anxieties and journey; and our magnificent ancestor Harriet Tubman, who now lives in the deepest recesses of my heart and the hearts of so many others. Together we will journey through time and space, past and future, to discover surprising new perspectives, timeless wisdom, and profound nourishment so we can meet the challenges before us today, within ourselves and in the world. As we embark on this journey, trust in the vastness of your own heart and you too will meet the spirit of Harriet. Her strong and resolute arms are wide open as she patiently awaits our collective awakening.

Spring Washam
Oakland, California
March 15, 2022

# Chapter 1

IIIIIIIIIIIIIIIIIIIIIIIIIIII

# A VISION OF HOPE:
# HARRIET RESCUES ME

I am running as fast as I can on some sort of road, and the wind is blowing hard. It's freezing cold and completely dark. I'm shaking, confused, and scared. I have an overwhelming sense that I'm being chased, but I can't see a thing, blinded by the darkness that surrounds me. I stretch my arms out in front of me and feel myself holding on to some kind of rope. Its coarseness is burning my fingers and palms, and I'm hanging on for dear life.

Over and over, I will myself not to let go, and I keep on running. I can smell the ground beneath my feet, and I feel throbbing in my ears—it's my adrenaline pumping. I sense intense anger in the field, and then I start to hear a mob nearby. Slowly rising out of the ground, I see shadowy images of slave catchers encircled by plumes of murky gray smoke. Dozens of them emerge, zombies with ghostlike, devilish faces contorted with rage. They're phantoms, some wearing strange symbols on their clothing, some carrying whips and others pointing guns. Then the sinister soundscape starts, men shouting furiously, dogs barking viciously, chains rattling, and the thumping of horse hooves pounding on wet earth. My senses become completely overwhelmed when I realize they're searching for *me*! Tremors of terror pulse through my body.

Somewhere in all the noise and confusion I realize I'm not alone, that I'm being guided. I am mystified when I realize that I am holding on to someone—another person—and they're running rapidly in front of me. And in the next shocking moment, I realize that it's Harriet Tubman! I am stunned and I feel a deep sense of relief. *What is going on?* I'm *actually* holding on to the back of Harriet Tubman's long, coarsely woven wool dress, and she's running swiftly, almost flying, and seems to know exactly where she's going. I absolutely *feel* the coarse fabric of her dress, my tight grip is what's stinging me like rope burns. Harriet, so used to being chased, so accustomed to evading capture, is guiding me with total confidence, and we're moving so, so fast. The danger is real, and all I can do is keep running. "Harriet," I plead loudly, "please get me out of here!" She turns her head ever so slightly and says, *"Yes, follow me, Child. I will show you the way out—yes, indeed, I will get you out of here!"*

When I opened my eyes and left behind this terrifying vision, my body was still trembling. I felt completely disoriented, and it took me a few minutes to remember where I was—a small house north of San Francisco that I'd rented while looking for housing nearby. It was just past 3 A.M. Night was still tightly wrapped around my room, and I was feeling suffocated by the darkness. I sat up, then walked slowly around the cottage, anxiously looking out each window for intruders and checking all the locks. My vision of Harriet and the slave catchers had shaken something so deep inside me that I began praying to every angelic being I could recall, including Mother Mary and Archangel Michael. Still deathly afraid, I turned on all the lights, pulled out some sage, and slowly walked around the house smudging and praying, *"Om Mani Padme Hum,"* calling on the Buddha of Compassion for protection and support. I kept going for a few hours, chanting and meditating, and finally as the sun rose slowly in the east, I began to calm down and feel safe viewing the kaleidoscope of shades of orange pouring through the windows.

That was spring 2020, and the world was on fire—the pandemic, police violence, the lack of justice, a growing white nationalist movement, all encouraged by racist rhetoric. I'd become incredibly weary of living in the underbelly of the American dream. It was all too much for me, and I had been preparing to move to Peru for the foreseeable future. In fact, I was heading to South America when the COVID pandemic hit, and all my flights were canceled along with all my scheduled retreats and plans for life in Peru. In a blink of an eye everything changed, and like so many, I had lost everything and was floating on the wings of anxiety and uncertainty.

Before arriving at that cottage, I had taken refuge at a magnificent mountain home of a dear friend while she was away. In the center of the living room was a majestic fireplace shaped by enormous round stones stacked all the way up to the ceiling. They reminded me of the sacred stones used in Native American sweat lodges and temescal ceremonies. Fire has always played an important role in Native American traditions, and it's regarded as a gift from the Great Spirit and a spirit messenger.

During those days of self-quarantining, I lay on my friend's sofa and spent hours upon hours alone just gazing into the fire. Then at night I'd create rituals, desperately willing my heart to come back to life. I wept and made offerings of sage, cedar, and incense, and I prayed for insight. Sometimes I would sing; sometimes I would dance; but mostly I just "gave the fire" my tears, the sorrows, the things I'd lost, my heartache for the world, the anxiety I felt for suffering beings everywhere. I was so disheartened I could hardly move; my body was collapsed in sorrow and frozen in fear. My time there became a long grief ritual and I quickly lost track of time as the days hastily turned into nights. I survived by chanting mantras and offering prayers for peace while the world was swept up in this pandemic of viruses, violence, delusional ideologies, and so much more. I prayed to the fire spirits to burn away my delusions, fears, sorrows, and anger, and to help me understand how I might find my center again and hold what was happening without being overcome by it all.

*What in the world am I supposed to do now?* I asked over and over, begging for a sign from the universe. I kept the fire lit morning and night, continuously feeding it giant wooden logs and watching the flames crackle and burn. And then one day something began to happen—the fire in the fireplace began to signal me and answer back. It was alive! Huge bellows of black smoke would rise and then suddenly turn white; it felt magical, maybe even miraculous in some way. Every day the fire and smoke would move in their own mysterious rhythm, popping and hissing, reminding me of a slow-beating drum. At times it looked like Morse code messages or smoke signals slowly rising toward heavenly realms. I had the deep sense that my heartfelt prayers for help were finally being heard. Fire symbolizes cleansing and renewal, and after weeks of fire rituals and oceans of tears, I was finally prepared to take the next step forward. It was time to leave and to discover where I needed to be and what I needed to do next. I knew I had to be of service to others at such a devastating time.

So out of the ashes of loss and despair came a glimmer of hope that somehow, I could rise to meet this moment. Now, reflecting on that time, I realize that Harriet was with me through it all. Although it was weeks before our first encounter—the vision of running away from slave catchers—she was already there with me, listening to my deepest prayers.

I didn't know it then, but this was the beginning of a collective awakening brought on by a series of painful events that unfolded with such orchestrated precision that I now marvel at the mystery of it all. A few days after the powerful dream with Harriet, I went for a walk with my sister, Hope. The cottage where I was staying was in the same town I'd lived in, on and off, for many years. It was where I practiced meditation, became a dharma teacher, and led meditation retreats; Hope lived nearby. *Dharma* is a spiritual word used by Buddhists and Hindus, and it means the truth of the way things are, or "like it is."

My beautiful sister and I were walking in town after a great hike in West Marin. Others were out and about, too, walking their dogs and enjoying the day. Hope and I were deep in conversation—I was sharing my experience with Harriet Tubman—when suddenly a car pulled up beside us and the driver, a white woman, just sat there looking us up and down. "Do you live around here?" she asked.

"Yes," I told her. At that point, I had no idea we were being racially profiled. It simply hadn't occurred to me. It seemed weird being questioned, but my innocence was still intact.

"What are you doing?" she asked.

I looked at her and said we were out for a walk.

"What are your names?" she asked. It was starting to feel creepy.

"Hope and Spring," I said, and she looked doubtful.

We were two Black women out for a walk. People were everywhere. Why would she question us? Yet she kept asking questions—my exact address, how long I'd lived there, where I worked, and where we were heading. Finally, I realized we were being racially profiled. Hope tried explaining that I was a meditation teacher who taught at Spirit Rock, nearby, but the woman didn't listen. She looked through us as if we were lying. Finally, I asked why she was asking all these questions, and she said there'd been break-ins in the neighborhood.

*Break-ins* was a painful trigger. My teeth clenched and I felt enraged. Ahmaud Arbery, a young Black man who was gunned down while jogging in his own neighborhood in Georgia, had been falsely accused of "break-ins." The story made national news and just that morning I'd posted his picture online and shared my feelings about this cold-blooded murder. I was heartbroken by what had happened to him, much of it captured on video. I felt outraged by this woman and her condescending interrogation, and I told her I didn't believe her and began to laugh. "Break-ins in this neighborhood?"

My eyes landed on a white couple walking nearby in peace. *Nobody thinks they're responsible for these break-ins. This is not right!* My mind raced, my mouth was getting dry, and I thought about Breonna Taylor, gunned down in her own apartment, shot five times by a police officer. I thought about all the Black people shot, killed, and brutalized over baseless accusations like this one. I had been teaching meditation in this neighborhood for years— leading retreats focused on loving kindness and compassion. There had been an article about me in the local paper chronicling my life and celebrating my work as a spiritual teacher. I had walked along this street many times, and my sister and I both lived nearby, yet this woman assumed that *we* were the threat to *her* safety.

It was so crazy that I grabbed my sister's arm and we walked away in silence. We stayed quiet for a long time. I know we weren't shot or even threatened with violence, but every Black person in America knows this feeling, that it's unsafe just *being*. That evening, neither Hope nor I brought up what had happened. Neither of us was ready to deal with the experience. So, as we sat together eating our Indian take-out dinner, we were quieter than usual; the sad incident was there hanging over our heads. I couldn't sleep that night; my body knew something big was happening.

The next day, on May 25, 2020, George Floyd, a 46-year-old African American man, was killed in Minneapolis while being arrested for allegedly passing a counterfeit $20 bill. Derek Chauvin, a white police officer, knelt on his neck for eight minutes and 46 seconds while Floyd was handcuffed and lying facedown, begging for his life and saying repeatedly, "I can't breathe!" During the final two minutes of the assault, Floyd was motionless and had no pulse. The heartlessness of the scene and the utter senselessness of his death were too much for me to bear. The incident brought me straight to my knees, and for several nights, I lay curled up in the fetal position sobbing, while images of George Floyd being suffocated and begging for his mother played over and over in my mind. I now believe that the reason I couldn't sleep the nights before Floyd's death was that my body knew something painful and traumatic was about to happen.

George Floyd's death, following on the heels of so much violence and so many shootings, punched my heart with so much force it literally knocked the wind out of me. It was just a day after my own racial profiling and worst of all, I felt a kind of terror and the sickness of white supremacy. *Is history repeating itself?* I felt shackles around my ankles, like we were being enslaved all over again.

Floyd's death was a modern-day lynching in broad daylight. Kneeling on a man's neck is painfully symbolic of the thousands of people who were lynched over hundreds of years in America. It's utterly symbolic of systemic racism and the oppression of Black people. Within 24 hours after the video went viral, it'd been shared millions of times. The impact seemed to hit like an atomic bomb, triggering a worldwide outpouring of grief, rage, and despair. Many friends and fellow spiritual teachers I know had similar reactions. Some were screaming, many cried all night long, coming to the realization that silence and inaction were no longer options. We were in the grip of another civil rights movement.

Hundreds of thousands of people took to the streets in protest, many with raised fists. Cars were honking their horns, and signs emblazoned with brightly colored words were *screaming* for justice. A fire had been lit, and many began to realize why it's so important to declare aloud that Black Lives Matter. George Floyd's death woke up the soul of a nation; it was a catalytic moment, an igniter, a moment of reckoning for America, and a wake-up call for the world to see the brutality that is inflicted daily upon Black and brown people. It was a heartbreaking moment, and I felt something huge shifting. The tectonic plates beneath our feet were breaking apart, and through this crack, Harriet's spirit emerged and began to soar once again.

During the long nights that followed, I continued seeing images of Ku Klux Klan members, slave catchers, and Nazis surrounding and threatening me. Every day, I'd wake up feeling a deep pain in my heart. I was more lost than ever: *I don't belong here. This no longer feels like home. This is not my place, not my country.* It was exhausting! Everything was spiraling downward. *O Lord, we are in troubled waters.* In these moments of deep despair, Harriet Tubman began to appear in my thoughts more and more frequently, and I began to reflect seriously on the dreams and visions I was having about her.

Until that first visionary dream, I didn't have much of a connection with Harriet Tubman. I watched the 2019 movie *Harriet* and studied about her in high school, but beyond that, I didn't know much about her. Then, after that powerful vision of her rescuing me, an incredible connection began to form. I felt Harriet Tubman around me almost constantly. When I closed my eyes, I saw her in my mind. I heard the name *Harriet* over and over. I felt her story coming alive in my thoughts and feelings. And I began to get interested in her life, reading everything I could find about her online.

Since fear and nightmares kept me up during those long nights, I started listening to gospel songs for hours and found them so comforting. It was church with old-school revival music, and it was powerful. "Ain't Gonna Let Nobody Turn Me 'Round" was my favorite, one of the anthems protesters sang while marching across the Edmund Pettus Bridge in Selma, Alabama, in 1965. I found myself traveling in time between this world and the world of my ancestors just by listening. Some gospel songs are so powerful that their sound vibrations can carry you to a higher place. When I was a teenager, I would attend Rev. Cecil Williams's Glide Memorial Church in San Francisco, and during their incredible Sunday services the choir would get to singing, and sometimes people would get woozy on their feet, shout spontaneously, or they'd just start dancing. The Creator would get ahold of them and their spirits would start traveling.

As the songs played on, I could feel Harriet's steady presence guiding me forward. I started praying out loud to her and asking her, my ancestors, and all the angels in heaven to lead me and my people out of this dangerous situation. It felt like I was walking in her footsteps, behind her and with her at the same time. Sometimes I could actually *feel* the subtle sensations and the pressure of her hand in my hand. I would get so energized by that, I'd stand up, grab my rattle, a hand-carved gourd with seeds in it, and start humming, clapping, dancing, and singing to the music. Something extraordinary was moving through me, and I knew that my ancestors and those old gospel freedom songs were awakening something deep in me. I had visions of another place and time with women singing and people dancing with tears on their cheeks. I began to slowly remember important things I'd forgotten, things I truly needed to understand about who I was.

I began to realize that Harriet was *really* with me, and I knew that she had rescued me for a reason. Words cannot describe the comfort, reassurance, and well-being I felt in her presence. *Harriet is here, and she is going to help me get through this. It's going to be okay.* I reminded myself of this over and over. Mama Moses was helping me find the faith and the courage I needed to keep on going.

# Chapter 2

IIIIIIIIIIIIIIIIIIIIIIII

# THE TASK
# IS GIVEN

A couple of weeks later, I'd gone from feeling lost to being "found." I stumbled across a magical tree house for rent in West Marin, a place where I could shelter and take refuge from the storm of 2020. It was near Spirit Rock Meditation Center, where I taught, and close to my sister and a few other dear friends. I desperately needed a place of my own during this challenging time. This small home was built high atop a hill on an acre of property, completely private and surrounded by old-growth redwood trees. Arriving there, I could only see these giant, majestic trees, and their huge roots, and I absolutely loved it. I felt safe and protected high up in my tree temple, and I surrounded the house with Tibetan prayer flags.

One day while meditating in my tree house, it dawned on me that others might be interested in Harriet and maybe others were having a similar experience to mine. As I shared my story, my friend Joselyn encouraged me to teach a class on the Dharma of Harriet Tubman and the Underground Railroad. So, I did. I organized a Zoom class to meet on five straight Sunday mornings. I had no idea if this would interest anyone, but I felt it was important for me to share Harriet's courageous spirit with others.

I posted a flyer on the Internet and sent it to my mailing list, and within a week and a half, hundreds of people had registered. These people were clearly interested in Harriet Tubman's life and how it intersected with the Dharma; my beloved assistant and I were flooded with e-mails from all over the world. I was awestruck and excited. Who would have imagined there were so many people as passionate about Harriet as I was!

Our Sunday online classes were overflowing with spiritual teachings, guided meditations, and gospel music. I shared the inspiring stories I was learning about Harriet and her Underground Railroad allies. I was bringing hope and inspiration to others, and to myself. I got to speak a lot, but so did others. There were so many wise people present, and I called on many of them to share their wisdom and experiences. What started out as a five-week class became a five-month "Church of Harriet Tubman" journey, and it carried us through the presidential election of 2020. Hundreds of people from all around the world brought their open hearts to our Sunday services, and during those two hours together, we laughed, cried, prayed up a storm, and then we danced. So many of us felt this deep connection with Harriet and were also feeling her magic and her power in our daily lives. We uplifted one another so much that we all cried when it ended. It was a multicultural, interfaith, intergenerational, international community. Those two hours each week for five months were beautiful, and downright holy.

I didn't know it at the time, but the vice president of my book publisher had joined my classes and she immediately reached out and asked if I would write a book about Harriet Tubman. I had serious doubts that I could, and I told her I'd need to pray about it. I prayed for a clear sign and three nights later I got an answer. I had invited my best friend Ali over for some prayer and meditation time. We lit candles and made offerings in front of my large statue of Quan Yin, the bodhisattva of great compassion. In Buddhism, a *bodhisattva* is an enlightened hero, someone who cultivates the "mind of awakening" and generates a wish to help all beings. Quan Yin is known for her deep listening; she hears the cries of the world and tries to help everyone. I read passages from the 8th-century meditation teacher Shantideva's great text, *The Bodhisattva Way of Life*. Ali and I talked about compassion and held hands as we prayed for the strength, courage, and wisdom to stay centered and resilient. We fervently prayed for all beings to be safe and protected, and we both felt a beautiful, celestial presence surrounding the tree house that night.

After Ali left, my heart was full, and my body was buzzing with energy from our inspirational prayers. I lay in bed and began reading *She Came to Slay: The Life and Times of Harriet Tubman* by Erica Armstrong Dunbar. While I was reading, I felt Harriet around me, and then after a couple of hours, still reading *She Came to Slay*, everything intensified. It was electric. The whole house began creaking as if people were walking on top of it. There was a high-pitched ringing in my ears, the air changed, the hair on my arms started to tingle, goose bumps appeared, and then my whole body began to tremble.

I closed the book and slowly shifted my gaze to the corner of the room, where I began to see a faint emanation of Harriet Tubman gradually emerging from the cool night air. She was revealing herself, slowly, bit by bit, until her spirit was completely visible to me. She didn't appear in a solid human body; it was a light-filled, unmistakable reflection of her exact image. Clearly, it was Harriet but in a spirit form. She moved toward me and was standing over my bed, looking at me, smiling and reaching her arms down toward me. I didn't realize I'd been holding my breath until I let out a long, loud exhalation. I was riveted by her emanation and the supernatural events unfolding in front of me.

I know without a doubt that we live in a vast, multi-dimensional universe, and I have had many mystical encounters and experiences while in deep meditative states. I have also had many experiences in the shamanic realm, so I'm comfortable with the idea of spirits and other worlds, yet I couldn't seem to stop shaking. It wasn't fear, but a response to the wondrous, palpable energy filling the entire space. I had never seen or communicated with a spirit outside of a sacred ceremony. I wasn't in a vision or a ceremony and I definitely wasn't sleeping.

Harriet sensed my nervousness and with a huge smile she said, *"Please don't be afraid, Springy."* Springy was my childhood nickname, used only by close family members. She wasn't speaking out loud and neither was I; we were speaking telepathically—talking without using verbal speech—mind-to-mind communication. I was completely overcome by emotion from her presence and her loving greeting. My heart was pounding in my chest, and tears were streaming down my face. She was so gentle, like the kindest grandmother, and at the same time, the high-voltage electrical currents that surrounded her were pouring waves of love into every cell of my body. It was challenging to stay present and in my body. The room became much warmer and very bright. It was like sitting in full sunshine on a summer's day.

I believe now that Harriet and I had moved into what Aboriginal Australians call the *Dreamtime*, a world in which ancestral spirits can talk to you. For Harriet to communicate with me that evening, my energy frequency needed to shift. Some people describe this as moving from the third dimension to the fifth dimension. Harriet had temporarily parted the veils between the human realm and the spirit world, which allowed my consciousness to synchronize with her exact coordinates. Through this temporary opening in the fabric of reality, we could, for a short period, interact very directly. Slowly, she began to explain that she had a very important assignment she wished for me to accomplish.

Harriet says, *"Child, your great task is to write this book about me and our journey together during this time. I don't need a scholarly book. We already have those. I want to talk directly to the people, to teach, to share, and to clarify who I truly am. I need to explain how things are and why I am back. I am needed here. My work is far from done."*

Her "in-person" visit that night was her opportunity to convey all her thoughts directly and to strongly encourage me to take on this significant task. I wasn't completely surprised, considering that my publisher had just suggested a book about her, and I had been fervently praying for a clear sign. It was all the unbelievable synchronicities that made the moment truly astonishing. She wanted the book not just to chronicle her historical life, but to describe our "sessions" together, in which she would talk and I would write.

Harriet says, *"Child, many books give dates and details about my life. These are important, but they don't share the depth of my heart. This book is about my heart, my feelings, and my thoughts. Through you, Child, I will tell a much deeper story. I have a message for the world, and your task is to help me share it."*

Everything began moving very quickly, and I became overwhelmed with the magnitude of it all. For God's sake, this was Harriet Tubman! "I'm not up to the task," I told her. "Please, Harriet, choose someone else!" I tried to tell her I couldn't do it. I told her of my fears of messing up, all the mistakes I could make because I wasn't ready for this. I told her no one would believe our story, this unbelievable journey we were on together. I told her I'd be called a fraud, a liar, maybe publicly attacked, ridiculed, and humiliated. I wasn't a scholar of African American history; I dropped out of college in my senior year. There were major gaps and blind spots in understanding my own biracial heritage. I couldn't stop shaking and I began to feel increasing levels of queasiness with the whole idea. "No, Harriet, please, you must choose someone else. I can't do it," I pleaded with her.

Harriet says, *"Child, you are the one I have chosen. All you need to do is move when the spirit says move and go where the spirit says to go. Everything will be shown at the right time, and everything will be provided to fulfill your part. We each have to do the piece our heart agreed to fulfill.*

*"I knew my task and I fulfilled it,"* she tells me. *"You do too, Springy, and our work, this book, is something we agreed upon a very long time ago."* With the warmth of a grandmother, she adds, *"Child, you* are *the one. You have the ability to navigate between worlds, to connect with the spirit world of the ancestors."*

When Harriet brought this up, I knew deep in my heart what she was talking about. I could "access" the spirit world; I had been accessing it my whole life, and now it was taking on an entirely new dimension.

That evening Harriet took me back in time and showed me some very important details I had forgotten, filling in many missing pieces. She reminded me that I always *knew* I was on earth for a specific purpose and that my life was, in a way, a training ground and that each experience was teaching me step by step. Until then, I would wake up some mornings deeply concerned that I was losing focus and wasting precious time; it felt like a dagger through my heart, as though I were breaking a contract that I didn't remember signing. Yet deep within me, I knew I had some big responsibility, I just couldn't remember the details. I would pray to Spirit, *"What is this great mission or task I'm supposed to fulfill?"* and at the same time, I was terrified to find out.

Harriet says, *"Yes, Child, you and I made this promise to each other a very long time ago. We both signed on to the deal and now the moment has come."*

Throughout the night I felt the deep truth of what Harriet was saying, and her words pierced my heart. I knew she was right, that I've always had a mission to fulfill, and since I was a little girl, I knew it was about the heart. Yet I felt frightened I would fail, or worse . . . let her down. "There's a war of self-doubt within me," I told her, continuing to shake.

*"I know,"* she says. *"Don't worry, Child. We all have to fight that fight. I'll walk with you and show you how to overcome it all, so you can speak, teach, sing, and conduct real magic."*

Harriet says, *"You only can do your part, my child. It's different for everyone. I chose the life I lived, to be a conductor, because I wanted to. I chose to run away from slavery because I had to. I chose to speak up because I was called to. I came into this world that way, Child, and I've been speaking up for a long time. We each have our own mission. We remember when we do, and it's different for every single person."*

So, very slowly, I began to accept that one of my biggest tasks in this lifetime was this undertaking with our great ancestor Harriet Tubman. There was so much I didn't understand, but by the end of the night, in the wee hours before dawn, in a shaky voice I finally said, "Yes, I will do it." Harriet said, *"We can go slowly. It's a sacred journey. We'll take it together."* And just like that our soul contracts written and signed so long ago were reactivated. The Akashic records were being updated and a new page was beginning.

Over the following days, while the world was locked down in quarantine, I was locked in a wrestling match with my personal demons. Harriet's faith in me triggered waves of painful feelings of unworthiness and self-doubt, and I began reflecting on why my self-confidence felt so low.

I believe it started with my childhood, which I can only describe as painful and sad. I was born in Long Beach, California, and my parents had little money, little education, and no access to emotional support to help them cope with the difficulties of life. Neither was prepared for parenthood and both experienced horrible physical abuses inflicted by the hands of their violent fathers. They both carried enormous amounts of unresolved trauma and I always felt immense compassion and empathy for them.

Their short, turbulent marriage was ending when my mother became pregnant with me. My father was addicted to the street life, and by the time I came along he had lost all interest in his marriage and his two baby daughters. He was constantly in and out of the house and his reckless and irresponsible behavior broke all our hearts. In a desperate attempt for a better life, my mother moved us north, and I lost all contact with my father for the next 22 years. As a young child I adored my mother, and it was her pain that made me interested in psychology. At just eight years old I began telling everyone that I wanted to be a psychiatrist so that I could help people with their minds. I am not sure where I first heard the word *psychiatrist*; however, I was always trying to understand the deep suffering of the adults around me.

Over the next few years, my mother, my sister, and I moved in and out of different houses and apartment buildings. My mother eventually fell in love with another deeply troubled man and that's when my life completely fell apart. She was determined to marry this abusive man, and I vehemently objected. It became a brutal war that I finally lost. I was forced to leave her home at just 15 years old. I remember the sad day when she drove me to the Greyhound bus stop and we stood looking at each other with tears in our eyes. I held a giant suitcase and a one-way ticket to Los Angeles, where I would live with a family friend. As I boarded the bus she waved, and I smiled back at her, trying desperately to act tough, as if leaving didn't matter to me. I cried for most of the 11-hour trip from San Francisco to Los Angeles.

Nothing worked out as we had planned, so I ended up living on my own in South Central Los Angeles, where I was surrounded by gang violence, drugs, and hopeless despair. Even in my worst moments, though, I knew somehow that my life wouldn't stay that way. I was all alone, yet I had this incredibly strong desire to live a spiritually based life and to help others, and it grew in me with every passing day. In my late teens I began going to a New Thought church. I studied psychology and joined the self-help movement. At 19 I was able to help myself overcome a debilitating period of depression by reading every spiritual book I could get my hands on and putting everything into practice. I always felt like I was being guided.

In my early 20s I encountered meditation—first in the Hindu tradition, then in the Buddhist tradition—which I believe truly saved my life. I always seemed to understand that freedom could only be found within the mind, and mindfulness practice gave me the keys to working with my suffering and my emotions in a direct way. I spent the next 10 years attending long silent meditation retreats, studying Buddhist philosophy, and learning under great Buddhist masters. After that, I spent years in teacher training programs at Spirit Rock Meditation Center and was lovingly mentored by my teacher Jack Kornfield. Leading meditation retreats and teaching classes became my passion, and in 2007, I became one of the founding teachers of the East Bay Meditation Center in Oakland, California. Our center was located right downtown, and this is where we brought social justice, diversity, and Buddhist philosophy together.

It was during that time, while I was trying to be a guiding light and to be of service to others, that I felt something was wrong. I took time off to do a three-month meditation retreat, and somehow the powerful concentration practice unlocked deeply suppressed traumas that I thought I had already worked through. This is not uncommon during intense meditation retreats; however, the emotional pain and inner turmoil caught me by surprise. It cracked something deep inside me and changed the direction of my life once again. I realized that I needed a new approach and a way to go much deeper. At the suggestion of a friend, I traveled to Peru in 2008 to begin working with indigenous Shipibo healers in the upper Amazon region of Peru.

I began spending months every year in the Peruvian jungle, learning how to heal my grief, my family tree, and the painful traumas still locked inside my body. When I returned to Oakland, I had the strength and courage I needed to lead our community. I would later spend a year living at a Shipibo healing temple where I apprenticed and learned everything I could about trauma, how to heal it, and how to transform it with the help of plant-based medicines.

It was there in the jungle that I also discovered that I had this capacity to navigate between worlds and dimensions. I'd had all kinds of mystical encounters during long meditation retreats, but there in the Upper Amazon region my experiences were welcomed and understood, and I felt very at home in that world. The local Peruvian healers began calling me *Maestra* and *Curandera*, words for "healer" or "doctor." I laughed it off at first, yet I was able to see and interact with the entire plant spirit world, and slowly I began to understand how to help people in their healing process. In 2016, I wrote my first book while starting an organization bringing groups of people down to the jungle to do healing work.

All this time, no one in my family really understood me or supported me in my work. My parents showed very little interest in my teachings, classes, and writings. For many years my parents remained distant, even suspicious of me, and often had negative reactions when I shared my insights with them. I did everything I could to express kindness, unconditional love, and daughterly devotion, yet nothing changed.

As I began my journey with Harriet, I finally realized that my family's lack of faith in me and their inability to feel my true heart were connected to the deep feelings of self-doubt now arising with Harriet. The demon of self-doubt is a powerful one, and I needed to overthrow it and believe in myself so I could move forward. I didn't know it then, but I would have many demons to battle while journeying with Harriet.

Even after I said yes to Harriet, I was still confused and doubtful as to why she would choose a Buddhist meditation teacher and shamanic healer to write this story. I wasn't an academic, I wasn't a powerhouse activist, and I was far from being one of those witty *New York Times* writers. I thought she should have called Angela Davis. "Before we start, are you absolutely positive?" I would ask over and over. She would just laugh and say, *"Child, I know exactly what I'm doing. You're much more than what you think you are. Trust me, Child, you are the right one. You'll see!"* Harriet was able to transmit great confidence, and I always had the sense I could climb Mount Everest if she was there by my side.

Slowly, over time, Harriet and I began to form a relationship where we could work together. I describe our times together as "sessions." Others might call it "channeling." If the idea of channeling is hard for you to wrap your mind around, you can think of my conversations with Harriet in a way that works for you—perhaps just being open to the idea that our ancestors and their consciousness live through us.

Harriet didn't need to show up in spirit form. Just through consciousness, we could communicate clearly. Some of our most powerful moments were with me sitting in front of my computer. In the beginning these sessions were incredibly difficult and took a toll on me physically. My body would shake for hours trying to release all the electrical energy that built up during the session. I'd be buzzing so much I'd become a giant ball of restlessness bouncing wildly off the walls, unable to settle down. At other times, it was the opposite, and our sessions would leave me exhausted for days. Being present with Harriet's spirit was like standing in front of a 747 jumbo jet at take-off—the power would just knock me down flat.

Little by little I began to slowly acclimatize to Harriet's high-altitude frequency, and I learned every day how to balance my energy to keep the flow of our dialogues smooth and intact. Long walks on the earth, power yoga, lifting weights, and taking good care of my diet were just the beginning. I felt like I was in a training program, like a runner preparing for a super marathon. Every chapter was an epic journey! Meditation, prayer, music, and earth-based rituals also helped me to stay present with her powerful energy and not collapse. But in the end what allowed me to adjust the most were my willingness to grow and my ever-expanding capacity to be present with my pain. Harriet's true story pushed every button within me, and my ability to compassionately hold all my emotions is what smoothed things out over time.

Some of our sessions lasted many hours; some were shorter. It was up to me. Harriet could go on forever; that's her nature. I would usually begin in the early morning with prayers and offerings at my ancestral shrine, having a large thermos of tea and enormous amounts of water that I consumed nonstop throughout every session. I'd surround myself with her photos—some were framed, and one was printed as a giant poster mounted directly on the wall in front of me. Seeing Harriet's image helped me open myself and invite her in. Then I would begin writing, sometimes with gospel songs playing quietly in the background and other times in complete silence. I knew the channel was opening when scenes from her life began to appear in my mind. Then I would see her face, and suddenly her presence would become very strong.

We always greeted each other with love, and she was incredibly patient. Each chapter was a journey, and as I wrote, the words, phrases, and stories would come through. I often needed long pauses to ask questions, clarify points, or just figure out how to write what I was seeing. She spoke not only in words but also through images, which really helped me understand what she was trying to say. It was like a children's book with words and illustrations on each page. She taught me very slowly—at the pace I could handle.

Sometimes I'd need longer breaks, like three to seven days, to process what she was trying to tell me or to research a topic in more depth. I began studying African American history in a way I never had. It was as though I was in a graduate program, and Harriet Tubman and Frederick Douglass were my professors. During these so-called breaks, I would spend hours watching documentaries, reading books, and studying about slavery, the Civil War, and the Underground Railroad. These are painful topics, and at times I would cry and feel like running away. When I took too long or ignored the call for a session during the day, I would usually be semi-awake all night dreaming of Harriet, and after those nights I'd wake up at sunrise to begin a session. Sometimes when I was washing dishes, sitting outside, or sending e-mails, my mind would slowly begin to fill with thoughts and images of Harriet, and that was usually the signal she was ready to go. I would grab a large cup of tea and my laptop computer and surrender to the process all over again.

Every day Harriet teaches me how to surrender—over and over, on deeper and deeper levels. Through her, I'm finding my strength, my voice, and some measure of courage, the kind of courage that's willing to risk it all. To lay bare my heart and try to give voice to hers still seems an impossible task, but it's the one I've been given and the one I try my hardest to fulfill. Harriet says she's ready, so let's go!

# Chapter 3

███████████████████

# GRANDMOTHER MODESTY AND THE FAMILY TREE

Harriet tells me, "*Start at the beginning*," and I reply, "Which beginning? Does the story start with your grandmother, who arrived on a slave ship, or further back than that? Where do you really come from, Harriet? Where does your story really begin?" I am full of questions. "*My real story goes so far back, Child, it's hard to keep it all straight*," she tells me. "*It goes back to even before everything existed, but we can start this part of my story with my grandmother.*"

Harriet says, "*Please don't go too fast, Child. Please slow way down. I want you to really know my grandmother.*" My mind rebels against this directive, and I feel my body bracing in anticipation of this painful story. The trauma of the Middle Passage is still very alive in the bodies of African Americans and other descendants of the African diaspora around the world. It's a compound trauma that involves not only slavery but also being brutally ripped away from your people, your culture, and the language you have spoken for centuries.

Many Black people in the United States and around the world are children of this African *diaspora*, which comes from the Greek word meaning "to scatter about." And that's precisely what the people of a diaspora do, they scatter from their homeland. Other immigrants to the Americas came due to wars, famines, or for economic opportunities. The African diaspora was different. These people were *stolen* from their birthplace, their motherland, where their ancestors had lived for thousands of years.

I confess to Harriet. I say, "The truth is, I feel scared to know Modesty, afraid that if I open to her, I might die of a broken heart. She endured so much. I try to imagine her as a beautiful woman walking freely and proudly on her own land, and that image makes me so happy. Then my mind goes to her kidnapping, then the horrific journey across the ocean chained on the bottom deck of a slave ship, and I feel myself getting sick."

Harriet says, *"Yes, Child, I understand. This is a door many are afraid to open, but we must.*

*"As you work with this chapter, it's important to take slow, deep breaths. You and everyone else reading this may want to pause and offer prayers of love and compassion to our African grandmothers and grandfathers. You best believe they can hear you; they can see you, and they can feel your compassionate heart."*

I allow myself to feel the hurt all over again as I travel with Harriet and her grandmother back in time; we are sailing across the ocean back to Africa. My mind fills with images of the vast landscapes, the red clay soil, the sounds of people laughing, families walking barefoot on the earth. I see the rich cultures, the ancient history, the traditions, the art, and the enormous sun shining brightly in the clear blue sky. I can hear the songs and I can feel the love and the dignity of the people singing them. I get so excited—these are Modesty's people!—and I see their happiness in who they are, and I experience their nobility throughout every cell of my body.

Harriet says, "*Go much deeper and really feel her. She is 'our' grandmother and she's alive in all of us. Child, the origins of mankind are in Africa. She has powerful medicine for our spirits when we are ready to take it.*" Harriet continually urges me to go deeper and to open to the idea that Modesty isn't just her grandmother and that she represents something far bigger. At first, opening to this feels counterintuitive— no one wants to feel pain—but then I feel a spaciousness in my heart and recognize how much Modesty's life *matters to me*. She was a real human being, and as I begin to love her, I feel deeper levels of love for myself. Harriet says, "*Yes, Child, in time you will begin to understand that she is you. Your earliest, primordial ancestor. You've taken the first step, just by opening your heart to her.*"

To truly understand Harriet Tubman, to connect deeply with her life and spirit, we need to begin by looking at what we know of her ancestral heritage. Our ancestors have a much more powerful effect on our lives than we know. The lives of our parents, grandparents, and great-grandparents are connected to who we are, because *they live through us.*

As a young child, Harriet was often told she looked Ashanti. The Ashanti are the largest subgroup of the Akan people, who live predominantly in present-day Ghana and Cote d'Ivoire. Prior to European colonization, the Ashanti people developed an empire and later the powerful Ashanti Confederacy, the dominant political and social presence in that part of Africa. The Ashanti were one of the few African peoples able to resist European colonizers and one of the few matrilineal societies in West Africa. They've always been known as fierce fighters, and between 1823 and 1896, Great Britain fought five wars against them, and it was not until 1901 that the British finally defeated them.

Some researchers now believe that Modesty was indeed taken from Ghana, and the Ghanaian government has welcomed her back home, proudly claiming Harriet as one their own. In 2005, Harriet's great-great-grandniece Pauline Copes Johnson went to Ghana on a historical and cultural fact-finding mission. There, she and her sister, Geraldine Mable Copes-Daniels, presided over ceremonies honoring the Underground Railroad heroine. Among other honors, a statue of Harriet Tubman was dedicated in the botanical gardens in Aburi and a street was named after her.

On the central coast of Ghana sits the Cape Coast Castle, constructed by European traders around 1652. It became the capital of the slave trade. Historians estimate that between 10 million and perhaps as many as 40 million enslaved Africans passed through those gates and the gates of 40 other fortresses throughout the region. These places had dungeons that could hold up to a thousand people each while they waited to be loaded onto ships and sold throughout the world.

Today Cape Coast Castle has been transformed into a sacred shrine honoring the millions of kidnapped Africans who passed through its gates. It's an important monument, a revered place to which thousands now journey on holy pilgrimages to reclaim the part of themselves that was lost and stolen. It's important that the seeds that were once scattered across the great oceans are now symbolically returning to be replanted one by one. People gather to walk through the dungeons, weeping and praying for the ancestors who suffered so terribly. They light candles, sing songs, and tell the stories of what they know about their family lineages. Many participate in healing rituals where they walk backward out the dungeon gates, symbolizing that the spirit of the person who once left Africa from this castle has finally returned to their homeland. These pilgrimages and ceremonies help to heal the traumas that we descendants of enslaved Africans carry in our bodies, even in our DNA.

Harriet says, *"Child, we don't have a lot of historical facts to go on, but what we do know is that the dungeon basement of one of those castles was probably the last memory my grandmother had of her homeland. She would have exited the 'door of no return' during her last moments on African soil."* Modesty crossed the Atlantic Ocean on a slave ship headed to North America sometime in the late 1780s. These crossings lasted about 80 days and hundreds of thousands of Africans died en route. Many boats sank and never made it. Countless people jumped overboard in desperate acts of defiance.

Harriet says, *"My grandmother would have been firmly shackled next to other men, women, and children forced to endure the traumatic, dehumanizing conditions as 'chained cargo,' packed together so tightly there wasn't enough room to sit up or move around. Neither was there ventilation, sanitation, proper food, or clean water. Women endured rape, and both men and women were whipped if they refused to follow orders. Their lives meant nothing to the people imprisoning them. This was a crime, Child, a terrible crime against humanity that went on for close to 400 years. This wound is so painful and so hard to heal because no one has ever been held accountable."*

The transatlantic slave trade began as early as the 1400s, when Portugal and then other European kingdoms were able to reach Africa by boat. The Portuguese were the first to kidnap or purchase people from the west coast of Africa and take them to Europe. Over time, it became a global enterprise and with it the so-called free-enterprise capitalist system was born, driven by greed. The small English colony of Jamestown, Virginia, set the stage for slavery in North America. On August 20, 1619, 20 or 30 enslaved Africans aboard the privately owned English ship *White Lion* arrived at today's Fort Monroe in Hampton, Virginia, where they were exchanged for supplies.

Harriet says, *"Child, 1619 is the year that kidnapped, living human beings became available for sale in America. This is an important date because it documents when the horrendous crime of slavery began on American soil. Folks need to know this date because it's a record of when this terrible sickness, a powerful form of evil, began rising in the consciousness of the people."* The name *1619* is also used for a powerful new educational program designed by Black educators. It's part of the growing movement to teach the truth about slavery and the full facts about American history within the US school system. I was surprised when Harriet used the word *evil*; it initially scared me. But then how else could one describe what happened to her grandmother Modesty and so many others?

The brutality of the transatlantic slave trade comes up regularly in my healing work with people of African ancestry. I and many others have relived aspects of Modesty's *traumatizing* ordeal on the slave ship with vivid clarity. It arises most powerfully during my shamanic retreats in South America. People will rock back and forth in rhythmical movements as if they are on a boat. Their uncontrollable wailing is interrupted by moments of sheer terror and unbridled hysteria. People report feeling chained, deathly ill, and unable to breathe. During these experiences, I'm there to provide loving support and a safe space to let the traumatic memories imprinted in their DNA go. It's nearly impossible to put into words the unbearable agony I personally experienced when reliving these types of memories. For a period of several months afterward, I felt genuinely broken. The enormous task of healing and reconciling this haunting crime has now fallen on the shoulders of a new generation.

Modesty must have been exceptionally strong, because she survived the long, painful journey through the Middle Passage and arrived in the Chesapeake Bay on the eastern shore of Maryland. It's hard to imagine how she was feeling physically and emotionally after finally getting off that ship. Standing most likely naked in chains on an auction block, unable to speak the language, she must have had no idea where she was or where she was going. All we know is that she stayed alive and was sold to a man named Atthow Pattison, a Revolutionary war veteran and the patriarch of a long-established Eastern Shore family that controlled vast tracts of dense timberland, rich marshlands, and productive farms. The only other facts we know about Modesty are that she lived on Pattison's 265-acre farm on the Little Blackwater River and that she gave birth to a beautiful baby girl who was to become Harriet's beloved mother, Rit.

After Modesty gave birth on that Maryland plantation sometime between the late 1780s and early 1790s, a powerful, new branch began growing on this family tree, one generation then another born in America. Harriet's mother, Rit, grew up working in "the big house" every day, cooking and cleaning, from the time she was 10 years old. She was considered the best cook around. When Ben Ross, Harriet's father, was purchased and brought to the plantation, he and Rit, who was still just a teenager, fell in love. Ben, an expert woodsman, managed the plantation's timber, overseeing the forests and estimating the value of the wood, skill sets that were highly valued.

Harriet says, *"Child, marriage between enslaved people had no official recognition, so folks created their own wedding ceremonies and rituals. Love will always find ways to bloom wherever it can, and my folks loved each other and got married.*" Harriet's parents somehow managed to stay married and devoted to one another throughout their entire lives. Together they had nine children: Linah, Mariah Ritty, Soph, Robert, Minty (Harriet), Ben, Rachel, Henry, and Moses. Harriet's official birth name was Araminta Ross, and they called her Minty. She was the fifth child, born in late February or early March of 1822.

Harriet says, "*Child, I realized at a very young age that my family was in a desperate situation. I came into this world ready to fight for freedom.*" When Atthow Pattison died, his daughter Mary and her husband, Ezekiel Keene, became the owners of Harriet's whole family, and these two families stayed locked in a karmic tangle for the next 45 years, altogether spanning four generations of Modesty's descendants. It was a sorrowful and painful dance between oppressor and oppressed. In his carefully recorded last will and testament, Atthow Pattison granted Rit her freedom when she reached the age of 45. She was to be freed at that time along with all of her children. But Mary had no intention of honoring her father's wishes, and Rit was never informed about the will or the promise of freedom. Somehow, though, Harriet knew that her mother and all her children were supposed to be free. Perhaps it was one of her premonitions, perhaps it was local gossip, but she knew, and this betrayal always haunted her.

Harriet says, "*You see, Child, the lives of slaves in the South are all governed by paperwork, and my papers were always missing, lost, or mixed up. It was like that my whole life. There was this great lie, and I always knew we were supposed to be free. There were days I just felt it in my bones; I felt it in my blood. I knew some great wrong had happened to my mother, and I wanted to find out the truth.*"

*"So, as I got older, I started doing jobs on the side and collecting small amounts of money. I couldn't read or write, so as soon as I got enough money, I went into town and gave it to a lawyer to investigate the papers about my family. To my utter heartbreak, I learned about the great lie surrounding our enslavement and freedom. Atthow Pattison had freed my mother in his will. When she reached the age of 45, she and all her offspring were to be freed.*

*"Atthow did the right thing by freeing my mama, and the fact that his whole family disregarded his last will and testament was such a betrayal, it took me days to recover from the truth of it. I'd boil over in anger when I'd see my mother toiling day after day, knowing she was supposed to be free. That was when I fully understood the wickedness of that family. I also realized no court in Maryland would hear my case. The lawyer said, 'A terrible wrong has been done to you and your family, and there's nothin' I can do to fix it. The court will not listen to you. Go back and stay as a slave.' As I left his office, I felt a deep knowing in my heart that I would free, not only myself but my whole family. The truth lit a fuse in me, and I knew in my heart it was just a matter of time before I would escape from these people."*

Because Harriet's grandmother had been so violently ripped away from her own family in Africa, Harriet went to great lengths to hold hers together. Her bonds with her parents, brothers, and sisters inspired many of her heroic actions later, as she became their greatest protector. Harriet says, *"My parents were very clever, and they figured out how to survive. Nothing made me happier than seeing my mother and father; they were so committed and so strong for each other. It's my family that got me through childhood; we were all very close. We helped each other get through the hardest of times."* The Pattisons committed every reprehensible offense you could think of when it came to Harriet's family, but she remained strong. She would not let this new branch of her family tree be destroyed. Her grandmother's sacrifice would not be in vain.

The topics of ancestors, family trees, and lineage are not ones we Westerners understand well. We weren't brought up to think about our place in a living lineage or how the land where our ancestors lived for generations is a part of our energy and our spirit. In indigenous cultures, though, ancestors, family trees, and what happened to our parents and great-grandparents are vital to who we become. Even though Harriet would never meet her grandmother or walk on the land of her ancestors, they were alive within her and within her strong and caring family. Maya Angelou often said, "I come as one, but I stand as ten thousand," and this refers to all our ancestors who walk with us and beside us.

Modesty seems to have mysteriously vanished after giving birth to her daughter. I ask Harriet what happened to her, and she reminds me of all the myths and African folklore about slaves being able to fly. These magical stories of flying Africans have been passed down from generation to generation. The folklore tells stories of slaves being able to enter a dream state and their bodies would lift into the air, carrying them over mountaintops and across seas. The spirit of the person would travel all the way back to their homeland, where they would regain their ancestral magic, spirituality, and power.

Similar stories are also told about water. There is the story of Igbo Landing—a site on St. Simons Island in Georgia where in 1803 a large group of enslaved people kidnapped from Nigeria rebelled and walked together into the marshy waters. They resisted being sold into slavery. They turned back to the waters from which they came to journey back to Nigeria. In these oral traditions, flying above and through water represented freedom and liberation. These folklores were very important for those in bondage; their ability to dream is what kept their spirits alive, it's what enabled them to survive. I love to imagine that Modesty had this supernatural ability and that one day her wings appeared, she soared up into the sky, and with the help of her ancestors she flew all the way back to her homeland in Africa.

In this very moment we can all honor her with a prayer.

---

## A Prayer

On behalf of Harriet's grandmother,
who represents all our grandmothers, I pray to
the Great Spirit, I pray for the healing of all the greed,
hatred, and delusion that would cause human beings to
harm one another in this way. By staying present with
all the suffering of countless victims and descendants
of the slave trade, may we bring forth the compassion
needed to heal this overwhelming trauma and pain.

---

# Chapter 4

IIIIIIIIIIIIIIIIIIIIIIIIIII

# HARRIET'S AWAKENING

When Harriet was born, her fate seemed a foregone conclusion, her destiny etched in stone. Just another Black child born on a slave plantation—condemned to live her life as a slave and die a slave. In the eyes of the law, she was a disposable piece of property. Her humanity simply didn't matter. That narrative was rampant, blindly believed, and brutally enforced by every slaveholder and nearly all of white society. That she was also born a girl added to the plot line, tipping the scales and upping the ante. She was valued even less. Nineteenth-century America was deeply patriarchal. Men held all the power and women, considered inferior, were excluded from voting or even owning property. So being born a Black, enslaved *woman* intensified Harriet's plight.

Harriet says, *"Child, being born a slave on that plantation nearly broke me. The conditions were so brutal, and slavery is just downright evil."*

In studying her life, I'm always awestruck that she was able to interrupt this tragic storyline and rewrite her own destiny so powerfully. At just five feet tall and 100 pounds, she was a force of nature, unstoppable, a woman who never believed what others saw as her limitations. She never bought into the "prisons of the mind" of either whites or Blacks. Even as a child and a young woman, she refused to accept the lies her owners tried to beat into her. She never accepted that being born Black and a woman made her inferior, unintelligent, or destined to be a slave. Harriet says, *"My body was temporarily imprisoned on that plantation, but they couldn't imprison my mind, my soul, or my spirit. Child, I was free a long time before I escaped from slavery."*

Much of what is known about Harriet's early life comes from her 1869 biography written by Sarah H. Bradford, *Scenes in the Life of Harriet Tubman*. I use this as a historical reference throughout the book. Outside of our formal sessions, Harriet gave me lots of guidance, reflections, and homework in the form of books. It felt important to familiarize myself with the historical period into which she was born and to read everything I could get my hands on.

Harriet says, *"I was interviewed for a few months about my life, and it was a good start. Many things weren't quite right; the writer left things out and I left a whole lot out. Child, it wasn't the right time to share certain things, because folks back then didn't know how to handle it. It was a different time then and many folks thought I was a fool. It's different now; the people are ready for what I have to say. NOW is definitely the right time to share everything. Let's start at the very beginning."*

Children born into slavery were, for the most part, shown little compassion. They were bought and sold and forced to work as hard as their parents. Little "Minty" had no childhood at all; her work began when she was a toddler. Harriet says, *"My mother had so little time for her family, so even as a tiny child I took care of my younger brother and baby sister all by myself. I was so small I could barely hold them up. I kept them safe and made sure that they ate, slept, and played. It was a time I enjoyed so much."*

When she reached the age of five or six, the Brodess family, her "owners," began to loan her to other white families to work, first as a nursemaid. She was ordered to rock a baby's cradle as the infant slept. When the baby woke up and wouldn't stop crying, Minty was whipped. Later she recounted a day when she was lashed five times before breakfast, scars she carried the rest of her life. The violence she suffered so early in life caused permanent physical injuries. Sometimes, she'd wear several layers of clothing to protect against the lashings. And at times, she even fought back. On one occasion Minty was forced to do housework all day and tend a baby all night. The beatings, cruelty, and sleep deprivation drove her to run away, the first of many times. She was six years old, and she hid in a nearby pigpen, sleeping with the animals for five long days. Hunger and thirst finally drew her out, and she returned to face yet another beating.

The Brodesses regularly loaned her to a man who forced her to check muskrat traps in the marshes in winter, and she became ill from standing in freezing water for hours on end. She developed a hacking cough, runny nose, fever, rashes, measles, and other ailments over and over; and she got to be so ill that she was sent back home. She'd return to the arms of her mother many times, and her mother would nurse her back to health, taking as long as needed, and then sadly, her owners would lend Minty out again. Over the years of being loaned out, she became so debilitated she was often bedridden and unable to work for long periods of time. The Brodesses tried to sell her many times, but when the buyers came to see her, they declined because she looked so deathly ill.

Then, a traumatic event stirred a deep awakening in her soul. Harriet says, *"Oh, Child, something so powerful happened to me, something beyond what I can understand, something I will never forget. When I was a young girl, I was sent to the store to pick up some provisions for the master. An enslaved man came running into the store with a terrified look on his face. He was being chased by the overseer. I felt sick, and a deep dread came over me. The overseer was carrying a large whip and he viciously grabbed the runaway slave. He screamed at me to hold the man down so he could beat him. I refused, and he picked up a heavy weight from the store counter and threw it at that poor runaway slave. It missed him and struck me directly in the head and broke my skull wide open. I was carried home severely injured and bleeding. Everyone was out working, so I was laid on the ground and left alone there for days. Everybody thought I was dying, and I went in and out of consciousness.*

*"I didn't know what was happening around me because I was traveling far beyond this world. It was the first of many experiences like that, where I would travel beyond this physical world into the world of spirit. In the other world, I could see and hear God as clear as day. It was God who brought me back to life, back into my body. It wasn't time for me to go, so back I came. But when I came back, I was completely different, and after that I became supernatural. I could hear, speak, and travel to distant worlds—into the heavens and back again. From then on I was living in two worlds, and a great burden lifted from my soul. I was Minty, yes, but I was much more than that. I had seen something.*

*"Somehow, I survived without even seeing a doctor. They forced me to go back to work even while the blood was still pouring out of my head. I wrapped a piece of cloth around my head, and I could barely see because the blood was flowing*

into my eyes. I was in a great pain, but inside I felt different—
permanently changed. All my fear dissolved away, and then
symptoms started cropping up. I would fall asleep while I
worked, sometimes standing up, other times midsentence. Even
the sting of the whip couldn't wake me. They tried to rouse me,
but it never worked. I would only wake up when Spirit was done
with me. I was a strange curiosity to everyone around me.

"Child, when I would go into one of my spells, I would be
journeying, traveling, as free as a bird flying out of her cage. I was
carried on the wind, wrapped inside the clouds of the most loving
and kind presence. In my visions, I would fly over the trees and
mountaintops, I saw Canaan Land, the ancient region between
the Jordan, the Dead Sea, and the Mediterranean, the land promised by God to Abraham. I saw the Promised Land, and I saw
that it was my destiny to go there. I could see all my people free,
no longer weeping, no longer in bondage, no shackled feet or auction blocks, and they were joyful. I visited lands where people
loved one another and worked together in a just way. I went to
lands with trees and hills so beautiful it took my breath away.
We ate good food, sang songs, and lived in harmony together. We
were glorious; we were beautiful; we were holy, living in peace just
as the good Lord wants all people to live.

"I stopped worrying about my health because I was shown
I would become very strong and everything I had been hop-
ing for would come to pass. Folks around me thought I was
a mad woman, but in my heart, I knew I was being guided,
cared for, and taught directly by Spirit. And I knew without a
doubt, I knew in my heart that I was supposed to be free, that
my visions were premonitions, I could see the future. I knew in
every fiber of my being that freedom was near.

"I felt a deep connection and a divine presence all around
me in every moment. I began to talk and communicate with
this presence every day. Child, after that I began praying

*continuously every day, while sitting, while walking, while eating, while resting, and especially while working. I began to pray and ask Spirit to keep me clean. If I was washing linen, I would ask to be washed clean in the same way. I sang songs and hymns and reflected on biblical stories while I worked in the fields. I couldn't read or write, but I heard folks reciting the stories of the Old Testament, and I understood them. It seemed I could call on this power anytime, at will, and my faith grew stronger each passing day."*

I ask Harriet, "What does *awakening* mean for an enslaved Black woman living on a plantation on the Eastern Shore of Maryland in the 1830s?"

Harriet says, *"I began to see myself in an entirely new way. I knew who I was. I wasn't just Minty anymore. I no longer saw myself as a slave but as a child of the universe, and I began to see that my life had great value and that my life mattered. I saw everything that I needed to do. I saw my task, and I saw all my previous tasks. I saw myself for the first time. A channel had opened, and through prayers and listening that channel got stronger and stronger. I began to know that this love is always around me and that nothing could take it away because it's who I am. It's who we all are, we just don't see it. Child, it's a powerful connection to your own spirit."*

She reminds me that her fight for freedom and her connection to a higher power are interwoven. Harriet calls this higher power God; others call it the Great Spirit, Christ Consciousness, Buddha Nature, Allah, or Shiva. All these terms refer to the loving intelligence that is all around us, an intelligence that has a thousand names. She shared openly throughout her life that she was in a constant conversation with a compassionate intelligence that pushed her onward, toward not just her own freedom, but everyone's.

I pause and look out the window. I'm in a tiny cabin in the Santa Cruz Mountains. I see a family of deer eating grass beneath the redwood trees. It's midafternoon, I'm sipping on a giant cup of black tea, reflecting on how to contextualize Harriet's life, her awakening, and the much bigger story behind it. *To really know who you are in the midst of whatever arises* seems a core theme. It sounds both overly simplistic and impossible at the same time. I'm not sure I truly understand what Harriet means.

Harriet says, *"Ask yourself the question, 'Who am I? Who am I really?' Meditate on it, pray on it, and then listen deeply."* Every time I ask, I go deeper until I begin to feel the vastness of consciousness, that it's all just energy and spirit.

"This is big," I say.

She says, *"Yes, Child, it's so much bigger than you know, and it's finally time to remember. This is the time to reclaim your magic and your power. It's all there within you."*

Aha! The first step is knowing in your heart who and what you truly are and not believing what's been programmed into you. Harriet says, *"Yes! Child, we are spirit, we are light, we are magic, we are just consciousness having a human experience. We have somehow just forgotten this."* When Harriet experienced her awakening, it changed everything. Her liberating insight into her true nature washed away a lifetime of false beliefs. This clarity allowed her to embrace her gender and her color and enabled her to break free—not only from those who physically enslaved her, but also from the internal prisons of the mind. It's the domino effect: If we knock down the doors to our inner prisons, then the outer prisons fall one by one.

It takes tremendous effort to wake up from the prisons of our minds. These are the falsehoods and fabrications we tell ourselves about the way things are, regardless of what's true and despite evidence to the contrary. These are the unexamined beliefs of cultural influencers, media, ancestors, parents, teachers, and friends.

Harriet says, *"I helped slavery get abolished but sadly not the mental prisons that went with it. Child, my spirit is alive and still conducting; but now I'm working for freedom through consciousness, through our minds, because that's where the real battle is."*

These mental prisons are the never-ending train of opinions and emotions that shape our lives and tell us who we think we ought to be. We believe that we have no power and that we don't matter. When these *beliefs* get deeply wired into our nervous systems, they become solidified into what I call *programs*, and it's hard to free ourselves from them. Even in the face of counterfactual information and when suffering the consequences of our misguided ideas, we remain loyal to these programs, no matter how destructive they are to others and, inevitably, to ourselves. Even though they create fear and unhappiness, we live our lives by these ideas and pass them on to future generations. They keep us lost and wandering, repeating the same destructive patterns over and over. These painful patterns are hardwired into us from birth.

Harriet says, *"Child, the programmed mind-prisons of anti-Blackness and white supremacy are two sides of the same coin. It takes two to dance, and when one person stops dancing, the dance is over. The jig is up. When one group stops believing and investing in the mind-made prison, the system begins to collapse."*

This is what we're seeing more and more of today as people participate in anti-racism work. This is what it means to "decolonize" our minds. We disrupt, unsettle, and pull out these unconscious programs. The disruption can begin with either the oppressor or the oppressed. When you believe you are superior, your job is to make others believe they are inferior. When you believe that you are inferior, your job is to live with internalized hatred and shame, which play out in traumatic ways.

In his beautiful book *The Water Dancer*, Ta-Nehisi Coates explains why a slave master had to keep enforcing the superiority-inferiority dynamic. When a slave developed pride, even if it was just in learning to read or write, they had to be beaten down repeatedly until the inferiority program was reset and fully internalized once again. In order for the program to work, it's necessary to destroy any sense of self-respect and self-love within the other person. The painful stories of slaveholders trying to break the spirits of enslaved people is beyond cruel. The *break* takes place when the victim separates from their own spirit and fully internalizes the white narrative. The break requires brutalizing them into accepting that they're inferior and ultimately into hating themselves. Today, progress and Black excellence evoke this old paradigm the most.

For 500 years, this sense of inferiority and destroyed capability for self-love has infiltrated Black psyches, communities, and culture—systematically and brutally enforced—and there's still unbearable pain around this program in communities of color all around the world. We've made phenomenal strides, yet for many this sense of inferiority—"You're nothing"—lives on and perpetuates itself generation after generation as deeply internalized self-hatred. We do it to ourselves, spreading it to our children, who live with bowed heads and a deep sense of shame for who they are. We are beaten physically, psychologically, and spiritually, and we beat ourselves in a painful cycle that's hard to break.

Harriet says, "*Child, you got to understand and remember this: All chains can be broken. It doesn't matter who you love, what your color is, your religion, culture, custom, or what kind of body parts you do or do not have. This love, this power, this intelligence is surrounding all of us. No one is left out. We all belong to it, and it belongs to us. Our deepest pain is believing we are separate from it, that it's outside of us, or that we're not worthy of it. We don't feel it, because we're asleep. We don't see it, because we're so damn blind, Child. But I see many eyes beginning to open. It's time, Child, it's time to see what's been there all along.*"

What made Harriet so powerful was that she unlocked the doors of these mental prisons early in her life. She woke up, and her message to all of us is to *wake up as fast as possible—there is no time to lose!* She is here to help us heal our old wounds by reminding us that we each hold great power. It's time, she tells me over and over, to move toward a future where our common humanity and the beauty of our multihued family is honored and cherished, and this begins within our own minds.

Harriet has become one of my great teachers, and she educates me every day about the nature of spirit, the power of love, and remembering who I truly am. When I am around Harriet, I feel the truth in what she is saying as if it's for the first time. We are so much more than we know! I am starting to feel it. Something big is shifting, and it's time for all of us to open the gates, wake up from the dream, and let go. My heart longs to be free; it longs for liberation.

## A Prayer

We pray that all beings everywhere
will quickly awaken and remember who
they truly are. We are light, we are spirit,
and we are children of the universe.

# Chapter 5

IIIIIIIIIIIIIIIIIIIIIIIII

# FAITH
# IN THE STARS

Harriet says, *"I had reasoned this out in my mind. There was one of two things I had the right to, liberty or death. If I could not have one, I would have the other."*

The North Star or Pole Star, also known as Polaris, is the anchor of the northern sky. It sits almost directly above the North Pole and has been there for 70 million years. During the night, it doesn't rise or set. It stays in nearly the same spot above the northern horizon year-round while the other stars circle around it. From the perspective of Earth, the whole sky rotates around it, which is why we can always look to Polaris to find due north. The imagery of the North Star as a prophecy of freedom has been passed down in many cultures from one generation to the next, and we're rediscovering through oral histories, legends, and myths its deeper symbolic and spiritual meanings.

The Pawnee Indians referred to the North Star as their "Chief Star," and they called a ring of stars in the heavens, connected to this star, the "Council of Chiefs." In Pawnee mythology, the Chief Star was sent by the Creator to watch over the people. It represented the governance style of their elders holding council to resolve important matters. The Pawnee set agricultural patterns and established social values in accord with the stars. They built their lodges with openings at the top, not only to allow smoke from the warming fires inside to escape, but to have a clear view of the Council stars, with the Chief Star shining the brightest.

The North Star is also associated with luck, because when you see it, it means you're on your way home. The ancient Greeks called it Phoenice because the Phoenicians used it for navigation. Throughout human history, it has been a powerful navigating tool for those in the Northern Hemisphere, helping sailors calculate their position and determine the course to their destination. Polaris is a lighthouse that helps all those traveling the seas at night navigate their boats safely to port.

To African Americans attempting to escape slavery, the North Star was a beacon of hope inspiring them along the road to freedom, beckoning them to the Promised Land. For millions in bondage, running away was a high-stakes gamble; their lives were on the line from the moment they stepped off the plantation. It was known among slaves that the North Star was the sky marker that could guide them north. They counted on the North Star to light their way to the free states and Canada, and despite all the risks, thousands made the effort.

The great abolitionist, journalist, and orator Frederick Douglass named his anti-slavery newspaper *The North Star*. He had escaped slavery not far from the plantation in Maryland where Harriet grew up. He was a few years older than Harriet and experienced the same brutality that she did. He established his abolitionist paper on December 3, 1847, in Rochester, New York, and developed it into the most influential Black anti-slavery paper of the pre–Civil War era. Frederick Douglass wrote of Harriet, "I have wrought in the day—you in the night. . . . The midnight sky and the silent stars have been the witnesses of your devotion to freedom and of your heroism."

In its deepest spiritual meaning, the lights in the sky and especially the North Star represent our own inner light—the light of truth, love, and wisdom. At times our light can be obscured like clouds temporarily hiding the moon, but its essence can never be destroyed. It takes confidence, bravery, and strong faith to follow the North Star, especially when we're lost and can see only the darkness. We can count on the North Star. It doesn't move; it's always there shining, helping guide our way when we can't see the way forward. Amanda Gorman writes, "For there is always light, if only we're brave enough to see it, if only we're brave enough to be it."

In all of our lives, there's a moment when we have to choose whether to be free or to die—to actually die or let our hopes and dreams die. It may sound overly dramatic, but for Harriet Tubman it was literally true time and time again. She constantly lived on the razor's edge between life and death. Runaway slaves who were captured received the harshest of punishments. Some were killed by their captors, many were tortured with whippings and beatings, even the chopping off of limbs or burning and branding of their bodies with fire. Some were forced to live wearing heavy ankle and neck chains, having their children and family members sold off, and sometimes being deprived of food and water for long periods of time.

Harriet says, "*Child, I had enormous faith in the North Star, and I believed I could follow it to reach the Promised Land, the free city of Philadelphia. I had visions of outstretched hands gesturing for me to leave the plantation and come north, and I prayed ceaselessly to realize my future freedom. My exodus from captivity meant embarking on a 120-mile journey on foot, alone, without money, family, or friends—and without a compass or a map, not to mention that I couldn't read or write. I estimated the journey would take four or five weeks to complete. Although I had a good chance at making it to the North, I knew I was breaking the law and that within hours of leaving the Brodess plantation, I'd be a fugitive risking recapture or death."*

This was Harriet's second attempt to escape. The first time Harriet was with her brothers, Ben and Henry. They took off together, but after several days of walking in the woods, her brothers began to fight with each other and with Harriet. They hadn't gone that far, and they were already too cold, too hungry, and too tired to continue. By this time, there was a reward posted for their capture, so they went back to the plantation. Harriet says, *"My brothers didn't trust my ability to get them safely north, so in fear and dread, they forced me to return with them. After that I made a solemn vow that I would never let anyone talk me out of what I knew I could do. I would never allow myself to be talked back into slavery."*

"But, Harriet," I ask, "how did you do it? How did you find the courage to escape again?" I was thinking about all the slaves who were recaptured or died. I thought about all the people at this very moment in refugee boats trying to escape wars and violence, many of whom drown or are sent back. I think of all the people stuck in detention camps at the U.S. borders, their only crime being their desperation for a better life. "Not everyone seems to make it, Harriet."

She says, *"Yes, Child, I know that. But you must be willing to risk it all for freedom. Many do make it, Child, and you must try over and over until you succeed. Better to die trying than to die a slow death in bondage, and that's all there is to it."*

People always underestimated Harriet. They viewed her as sickly and weak, especially after her head injury and her habit of falling unconscious. Harriet's visions of God and the Promised Land weren't taken seriously, not even by her husband, John Tubman. She and John were married in 1844, and their marriage lasted about five years. He was a mixed-race freeman who lived near her father's place. They were unable to have children, and even if she had given birth, the children would likely have been taken from her since she was a slave. John never believed in Harriet's visions and found her sleeping spells strange. In spite of being a freeman, he refused to go to Philadelphia with her, which she found heartbreaking.

Harriet says, *"I knew in my bones I was strong enough to make the journey alone. I spent years from sunup to sundown doing the hardest labor, chopping trees and hauling heavy timber through the forest. As a child and teenager, the constant beatings, malnutrition, and other injuries left me so ill, Child, I just about died more than once. As I grew older, though, my body became incredibly strong, and I was able to work harder and faster than all the men around me. I was proud of my strength and my muscles. Working in the forest was work I enjoyed, because I was often left alone, far out from the 'big house,' moving my body and breathing fresh air. It was a great relief."*

Becoming familiar with the forest, the back roads, and the landscape all around her was an important skill set that would help Harriet on her arduous journeys. As a child, she loved being in the forest alone, far away from the master's house and from the overseers. She experienced a deep sense of peace and felt completely at home in the woods, and this feeling grew stronger as she entered adulthood. Harriet says, *"I spent years wandering the backwoods of Maryland and I developed a deep connection to the plants, the trees, the rivers, and to the natural world. Over time I became quite the herbalist. I discovered many healing medicinal plants, and somehow, I always knew exactly how to use them. It was a great gift, Child, because I could help myself during my journey, and later I was able to help others and even save lives."*

It was during the fall of 1849 when an inner voice began whispering to Harriet, *"Arise, flee, escape!"* She was about 27 at the time and dreamed every day of leaving. Living as a slave on that Maryland plantation was getting more and more dangerous, especially after her first escape attempt. The Brodess family's fortune was dwindling, and there was talk of selling her and her brothers to slave owners in the Deep South, where conditions would be even more difficult and harsh. So Harriet felt an urgency to run away as soon as possible. Her uncanny ability to see the future always seemed to keep her one step ahead of danger. She began to have recurring visions of horsemen coming after her, and she heard the shrieks of women and children being torn apart. The time had come, and she said good-bye to her family and friends for good. Her mother sobbed when she saw her heading out. Harriet stopped at the cabin of each family member and sang a song.

*I'll meet you in the morning,*
*when you reach the Promised Land*

*On the other side of Jordan,*
*for I am bound for the Promised Land.*

For Harriet it was her time, and when the sun disappeared beyond the horizon, she disappeared with it. Her journey to go *into the wilderness* by herself was both literal and symbolic. In shamanic cultures, wilderness represents power and wisdom, but it comes at a steep price. It represents the underworld of our unconscious minds, the places where we're stuck and lost. It's the arena, the battlefield, where only the strongest warriors survive.

I remember on my first trip into the Peruvian Amazon I was scared to death, but I knew I had to go. So, off I went alone to face myself, to confront my fears and reclaim some part of myself. I entered the *dance of no hope* alone and once it began, it was out of my control. I was forced to surrender everything to a higher power. I had to surrender it all to have any hope of making it to the other side.

Without a doubt this 120-mile journey was Harriet's initiation, her rite of passage, and it brought with it life-threatening challenges. It was sometime after October 3, 1849. Standing at the crossroads, she saw the long path ahead as a stepping-stone, a sacred threshold she had to cross. Like many brave souls before her, Harriet followed the North Star, which she located by finding, first, the Big Dipper (which, according to lore, enslaved people called the *Drinking Gourd*). With this sense of direction, she spent long nights scaling mountains, wading through rivers, and moving through thickly forested areas. During the daytime, she'd hide as far as possible from the main roads. Then, all night long she walked and walked, gazing up into the dark sky, guided by the beaming and twinkling of Polaris. It was as though the heavens themselves were trying to guide her to safety, to lead her through the darkness, out of the wilderness, and finally to freedom.

During the long, cold nights, the stars, trees, and hooting owls kept her company, and she strode farther and farther into the unknown. She walked alone praying, and when she grew just too tired, she lay down on the icy ground to sleep. Harriet says, *"I prayed for guidance with each step. I prayed when I was dog-tired. I prayed when my feet were bleeding. I prayed for the strength to keep going when the pain of hunger got to me. I prayed when my head throbbed. I prayed for warmth when I was cold and shaking. I prayed to avoid the slave catchers who were looking for me. Child, one day I noticed that all my prayers were being answered. Faith is the light we follow, an inner confidence that we can do it and that we are being guided."*

At key moments along the way, Harriet did receive some much-needed help. She didn't know who she could trust, yet she was always guided to the right people for food; and when she desperately needed a warm shelter, it always appeared. We know that many Quakers and abolitionists assisted runaways and helped them on their dangerous journeys to Philadelphia and New York. This was her introduction to the "underground" movement, the resisters and the interrupters of the status quo, the abolitionists who were so fiercely dedicated to abolishing slavery that they put their own lives at risk to help runaways. It was through them and the guidance of the North Star that she was able to reach Philadelphia. Harriet would never disclose who had helped her connect to the Underground Railroad. It's likely she swore an oath, and Harriet never broke her vows.

Harriet says, *"Oh, Child, I never gave up, no matter what happened. Folks give up way too easy now. They have a few challenges or people try to stop them, and they give up on themselves.*

*You got to believe in yourself, even if no one else does. You got to believe in yourself, even when folks try to beat you down. You got to believe that you have power, even when folks say you don't. Every human being has a light inside that no one can ever take away. They can't steal it out of you, they can't beat it out of you, and even if they kill you, it goes with you. It's yours, Child. It's this light that keeps me going, you see. It's so strong it can break down the inner barriers. I am not sayin' it's easy, but what I am saying is that if you're willing to stay the course and not give up, whatever is in the way will eventually move."*

Harriet's visions, her confidence, and her devotion were all bolstered during her daring escape. Initiations are always rigorous and intense, yet at the end we are given the gifts we've heroically earned. She was starting to use and embody her gifts, and her faith in herself became stronger because of it. Even her terrible headaches, fainting spells, narcolepsy, and seizures didn't stop her; they just spurred her into deeper and deeper mystical states. Her supernatural abilities to *know*, *see*, and *hear* things that others couldn't were beginning to set her apart. This, along with her courageous heart and fierce will to live, is why we respect and honor Harriet Tubman so deeply.

Like her grandmother Modesty, who survived the horrific Middle Passage ship ride from Africa, Harriet too survived a treacherous journey. Running away victoriously and claiming her God-given right to be free was a defining moment in her life, a genuine turning point. Harriet says, *"Child, my journey wasn't just for me alone; it was for my family, ancestors, descendants, and for all those who weren't able to make the journey. All my ancestors were with me when I finally crossed that line into Philadelphia. It was truly a joyful moment, Child, one I will never forget."*

◆

*When day comes, we ask ourselves.*
*Where can we find light in this never-ending shade?*
*The loss we carry, a sea we must wade.*
*We've braved the belly of the beast.*
*We've learned that quiet isn't always peace.*

— AMANDA GORMAN, "THE HILL WE CLIMB"

❖

## Chapter 6

# HARRIET THE CONDUCTOR

*"Read my letter to the old folks, and give my love to them, and tell my brothers to be always watching unto prayer, and when the good old ship of Zion comes along, to be ready to step aboard."*

— Harriet Tubman

On one powerful occasion just after an especially deep and touching writing session with Harriet, I took a break from my laptop computer and sat on the spacious deck beneath the giant redwood trees that surrounded my home. It was a beautiful summer day, early afternoon, sunny and warm. It was quiet except for the sweet melodies of the birds chirping around me, the crows squawking in the distance, and the rustling of tree branches high in the sky. I was sitting comfortably on a lounge chair with a straight back, bare feet, and my legs stretched out in front of me. I folded my hands on my lap, gently closed my eyes, and fell naturally into a very still and meditative state. Within about 20 minutes, I began to feel strong sensations in both my legs and feet. It was neither unpleasant nor pleasant, just throbbing, pulsating, and vibrating, and as it intensified, I wondered if my legs had fallen asleep. I stood up and my body began moving instinctively. Some inner impulse took over and I gradually began to walk slowly in place. I felt my body moving intuitively on its own, like I was on an invisible treadmill.

Then I began to feel a different kind of strong energy that I can only describe as overwhelming compassion and empathy. It came in waves and struck my heart over and over, making me weep, sometimes uncontrollably. While tears were streaming down my cheeks, I could hear singing—hauntingly beautiful, soulful songs along with the sounds of heartfelt prayers, and Harriet was singing with them. I had entered a powerful vision. "We" were all walking in single file on an earthen path with worn-out shoes, no laces, no soles, busted boots, torn socks, with bandages on our bloodied and blistered feet. I could feel all their emotions like faith, worry, despair, and the deepest longing and dreams of a new life. I felt it all inside my body as my feet became their feet. We walked on and on singing and praying, men carrying large bags on their heads and women carrying children and baskets in their arms. This was Harriet Tubman's Caravan of Freedom, and it was full of hope and optimism. They were walking through darkness, walking through fear, and walking with Harriet as she led them toward their new life.

I still get emotional remembering that experience; the poignancy was just so moving, beyond what words can convey, but I'll try. Harriet was sharing short energetic glimpses of her spirit while she was conducting on the Underground Railroad. Through her and through me I felt for the briefest of moments what it was like on the Railroad. It was like seeing a memory, but I wasn't just seeing it;

I was reliving it and experiencing it somatically—through my entire body—while simultaneously being present in this moment.

I ask Harriet, "What was that? What happened to me there?"

Harriet says, *"Child, we went back in time so you could get a real feel for my spirit and a good sense of what it was like walking with me and a group of passengers I was conducting."*

I say, "Oh my God, Harriet, I could barely handle it."

Harriet says, *"I know, Child, the waves you describe hitting your heart was my energy. I know it's strong. You experienced this vision because it's real. I want you to 'feel' what we're talking about, not just think about it in your head. I showed you just a few minutes because that's all you can handle. This is no myth, Child, this is American history and the legends surrounding the Underground Railroad are true. I been there; I know what it was like."*

It took about two days before my body stopped shaking and the pressure on my heart and chest eased. The experience was not just heart-opening, it was life-changing. Something shifted inside me, and it helped me grow. I'd gone back in time and could feel my spirit in Harriet's world; and my admiration and devotion for her grew exponentially. I stopped wasting time with silly questions and began to interact with her less casually and in a more respectful and honorable way, as I would with any authentic spiritual teacher. Harriet was a real conductor, leader, and guide on the Underground Railroad. Everything about her was becoming more and more real.

Harriet says, *"Oh, Child, being a conductor is a spiritual calling, and I did everything because of love. It's important folks know this about me. I love our people, and it was my heart that led me to conducting on the Underground. Many of the rescues* began with visions that someone I loved dearly was in danger of being sold or killed. Love is what kept me doing what I was doing. I hope you can feel my heart, Child. This is what conducting is all about."

I laugh and say, "Yes, I can always feel your heart, that's for sure!" And that's the honest truth; I always feel love surrounding Harriet, even to the point of my energetic circuitry being blown to bits. I feel her superpowers too, but her tremendous love and incredible warmth are always there.

Harriet's situation after making her way north was both bitter and sweet. Harriet says, "At the very beginning when I made it all the way to Philadelphia, I felt pleased, and I was in high spirits. Before long, though, I began to feel a deep loneliness and a great burden on my heart. I was both free and not free. I was a wanted fugitive, and I was alone without my people for the first time. There was no one to welcome me to the land of freedom. I was a stranger in a strange land, and my home after all was down in Maryland, because my father, my mother, my brothers and sisters and friends were all there. My family was still enslaved, vulnerable, and in danger. They could be sold at a moment's notice. The thought of it was too painful to bear most days. I was free, and they should have been free too."

A deep stirring began to grow in Harriet's heart. She was beginning to feel the suffering of *all* the people who were still enslaved. Seeing the lively free Black community in Philadelphia was a constant reminder of those left behind, and her dreams of bringing her whole family north took on a deeper urgency. She found work as a domestic servant and began saving all her money. *"I am not free until we all are free."* These words were a constant reminder to her, and it became a sacred mantra that she repeated over and over as she prayed and contemplated what to do next.

Soon she learned through her network of friends on the Underground that her niece Kessiah was slated for the auction block in Maryland, and Harriet sprang to life. This would be her first mission and the beginning of her 10-year odyssey as a conductor. Her niece, now 25, was for sale along with her six-year-old son and newborn daughter. There was no guarantee they'd be sold together. Harriet knew she had to intervene; she was determined to break these generational shackles.

The other Underground Railroad agents tried to talk Harriet out of conducting operations. They had never seen a woman conduct missions, and at first, they thought it was senseless and that she might be delusional from her head injury. People always underestimated Harriet Tubman because of her small size, her gender, and the fact that she was uneducated and unable to read. But none of that mattered to Harriet, even the dangers. No one knew what to make of her, but it wouldn't be long before they were all bowing their heads in deep respect for the woman everyone began to call Moses.

Harriet says, "*Child, public slave auctions took place in the middle of town squares with crowds of people watching. White families out shopping and buying their fruits and vegetables next to 'shoppers' poking and prodding the bodies of living human beings in chains. Children eating their picnic lunches and mindlessly playing games in the middle of this inhuman spectacle was just sickening. Women were often examined naked, and buyers could touch and evaluate their genitalia before they made their bids. Child, nothing was off-limits, and children were often yanked right out of the arms of their crying mothers. The separation of families was one of the worst aspects of slavery. It hurt me to my core when my sisters were sold off. This emotional damage, this pain, is still alive in the Black community today; it's far from healed."*

Harriet had power now, and she was intent upon using it to save her niece Kessiah and Kessiah's two children. Harriet set out from Philadelphia, traveling by night in extreme secrecy, and spent days walking alone back to the plantation in Maryland to organize the escape. Kessiah had two things going for her. First was her Aunt Harriet and second was her devoted husband, who not only was a freeman but was more than willing to risk his life for this mission. They worked strategically together with the Underground Railroad agents. Harriet helped Kessiah's husband secretly purchase his wife and children; then he smuggled them out of the jail cell where she had been placed for the auction. Guided by Harriet, they all traveled from house to house along the Underground Railroad until they arrived safely in Philadelphia. Harriet says, *"Oh, Child, I was overjoyed to finally have some of my family free! After successfully rescuing my niece, I felt a power I hadn't known before. I was ready now, confident that I could help free others from bondage. So once again I decided to travel back to Maryland to rescue other family members and friends."*

The Underground Railroad operated between about 1810 and 1850, and possibly for as long as 65 years by some estimates, and 100,000 slaves traveled the Railroad to escape from bondage. It was incredibly well organized, with as many as 60 stops, designated meeting points, secret routes, various forms of transportation, and safe houses along the way. The stations were known as depots and were mostly the homes and businesses of white families. Some stations were legitimate businesses that were open to the unsuspecting public during the day, and others were private homes of abolitionists and sympathizers. The stations were run by "station masters" or "agents," who took great risks; not only were they providing food, shelter, and supplies to runaways, but they were also passing secret messages back and forth using coded language—often in the form of poems or songs—to alert the next station master about the arrival of the group.

Harriet says, *"The most important role in the success or failure of a rescue mission was that of the conductor. Child, this was dangerous business, I was responsible for keeping the entire train 'on track' as it moved north. If I made one wrong move or one bad decision, it could put everyone's life at risk. I was a good captain because I had strong determination and was able to overcome all the roadblocks we faced. Child, I was able to avoid police, dogs, mobs, bounty hunters, and slave catchers. I was the person responsible for guiding everyone to safety, and I took it very seriously."*

Once she started conducting a journey, she was relentless, and would never consider giving up or stopping. On one mission, she threatened to kill anyone who lost their nerve to escape. She told one man while pointing a gun at him, "You go on, or die." She couldn't risk him getting caught and telling what he knew. I ask Harriet about that experience and what it was like leading the groups, especially while carrying a loaded pistol.

Harriet says, *"Oh, Child, I was downright ferocious in those days. I had to be wrathful"*—she chuckles—*"but that was just on the outside. I was like a panther. A panther looks fierce, even in a relaxed position, because that's its nature. It was born looking fierce and so was I. But when you see a panther with her cubs, you see a soft side as well. While I was conducting on the Underground, I had to shapeshift into the most ferocious black panther you can imagine. But, Child, I always had a very soft side."*

Harriet led her groups through swamps and forests, across mountains and rivers, amid rain, thunder, and huge snowstorms. They needed the cover of darkness, so most of the missions were done in the winter months when the nights were longer and daylight hours shortest. Avoiding frostbite and staying warm were a constant challenge. During the days, they hid in swamps, caves, and Underground safe houses. At night they traveled on foot, walking and even running for miles until the sun rose. Some routes were only a hundred miles long; other journeys covered 800 miles and took up to six weeks on routes that wound through Maryland, Pennsylvania, and New York, all the way to Canada.

Harriet says, *"Sometimes I had to guide passengers through very dangerous places and at times it seemed we'd be caught. I would fall into spells and trances and when I woke up, I could see the next stop and know just how to get there. All conductors learned quickly that routes can change in the blink of an eye. When I was in real need of help, I used songs, whistles, and owl calls to signal station agents in the dead of night. Often, Child, I would just start praying, and miracles would happen. My prayers were often answered by Quaker families who would magically appear out of nowhere to offer aid in the form of food, water, clothing, medicine, or, most important, shelter when we were being hunted down and in serious danger of being caught."*

Although escaping slaves were assisted along the way by free Blacks, former slaves, and Native Americans, it was primarily white abolitionists, many of whom were Quakers, who had the funds, freedom of movement, and the fortitude and belief to be at the forefront. While she was still alive, Harriet said, "Quakers almost as good as colored. They call themselves friends and you can trust them every time."

Harriet's nickname Moses began as her Underground agent code name, and it gained steam when abolitionist William Lloyd Garrison referred to her as "the real Moses." Harriet says, "*My passengers called me that because I would sing songs about Moses* [like "Go Down, Moses" and "Bound for the Promised Land"] *and make biblical references to signal when I was coming and when the train was leaving. I would change the tempo of the song to indicate whether it was safe to come out or not. Child, I still have a powerful connection with the story of Moses and the Old Testament Bible stories. While conducting, my passengers became the Israelites enslaved in Egypt, and I was their Moses carrying them to the Promised Land.*"

As the legend of the new Moses grew, people assumed this great liberator was a man, and many were shocked to find out this Moses was a woman. Harriet says, "*Oh, Child, there were rumors everywhere in Maryland about some person leading slaves north. Whole families were disappearing overnight, and the slave owners were becoming outraged and confused as to who was stealing their slaves. At first the slave owners were calling me the "black ghost." Folks—both Black and white—could not believe that a woman was leading large groups of slaves all the way to Philadelphia.*"

Harriet seemed to possess a magical ability. She could put on a "cloak of invisibility" and be able to hide in plain sight, sometimes walking in broad daylight right beside her wanted posters. She was still a wanted fugitive. Harriet says, "*Child, I knew a higher power was guiding my life, and I also knew I was a wanted fugitive with a bounty on my head. It wasn't far from my mind that I could be apprehended and taken back into slavery at any moment. So I had to be very careful when traveling on trains and visiting different plantations.*"

For this she used a variety of disguises, sometimes as an educated, rich lady and other times as a disoriented slave girl carrying chickens. She used false IDs and forged documents to make her way south on the trains. Everything was organized by the Underground alliance.

In one of her most daring rescues toward the end of her conductor years, she was able to rescue both her mother and father and get them all the way to Canada. Harriet says, *"I refused to let them die on that Maryland plantation, especially after I had a vision that my father was going to be arrested for aiding and abetting slaves to leave. I leaped into action and organized that mission with the help of the Underground."* She was completely devoted to her parents, and she was desperate to reunite them with the rest of the family she'd already rescued, who were now residing in Canada. Their advanced age made it a difficult trip, but she felt certain at every moment that they were divinely protected. Harriet says, *"I walked with them all the way to the Canadian border to start their new life. Oh, Child, that was a blessed day!"*

Harriet made 13 trips back to Maryland and rescued close to 70 people, including the majority of her family members. She was unable to rescue three of her sisters, who had been sold and transferred to the Deep South. Harriet famously once said, "I was the conductor of the Underground Railroad for 10 years, and I can say what most conductors can't say—I never ran my train off the track, and I never lost a passenger."

Her life as a conductor was far from easy, and it would sometimes take her months to recover from these long missions. I don't think we'll ever know exactly how many people she helped and inspired along the way. Her legend spread like wildfire and inspired countless others to escape to the north too.

It was one of Harriet's most trusted friends, William Still, who helped introduce her to the world. Known as the "Father of the Underground Railroad," he was a brilliant, fearless Black abolitionist based in Philadelphia. He himself was a conductor, businessman, writer, historian, and civil rights hero. He interviewed each escaping slave and kept meticulous records, including a biography and the intended destination of each one, along with any aliases they went by. It's thanks to him that we have so much information about Harriet's unbelievable journey in her own escape and as a conductor. He archived every step of her way. They also collaborated on many missions, and she passed through his office with rescued passengers many times throughout the 1850s. He used these detailed records to write an account about the Underground Railroad and the experiences of many ex-slaves titled *The Underground Railroad Records*, published in 1872.

For a while, I would pretend to walk in Harriet's shoes, but now I just bow down to her, humbled in deep respect. Good Lord, those are some huge shoes to fill. Her spirit was Moses back then and she is my Moses now. Her unbelievable courage, deep abiding faith, and all her heroic actions are why we are still talking about her now. As I write these words, many people are walking the same path that she did in Maryland on a pilgrimage to connect with her spirit. I believe in her magic; her essence and life force are still there. They start on the Tubman Byway in Dorchester County, Maryland, and walk a hundred miles in her footsteps, tracing her route along the Underground Railroad. More and more groups are feeling the call to walk this path to understand who Harriet Tubman truly is.

The Underground Railroad is alive today. It's not just a symbol of freedom; it also represents our expanding consciousness, a new awakening, and a higher perspective. Something is happening and, through Harriet, I'm starting to feel that something much bigger than I can understand is unfolding. It's both mysterious and exciting!

Harriet says, *"Yes, Child, something big is happening. You'd best believe that I am still a conductor on the Underground and all you need to do is say yes when the time comes. I will take you and anyone else who is ready to go!"*

# Chapter 7

## THE INNER UNDERGROUND AND THE PROMISE OF FREEDOM

Around this time, my conversations with Harriet started to change in unexpected ways. As she began sharing more and more of herself, her voice changed from that of a wise grandmother to the voice of a great spiritual teacher. It took me by surprise, and I was astonished by the depth of her wisdom and the new ways she would convey her thoughts. Early one morning while I was sipping a giant mug of black tea, I had a profound session with her, revealing the brilliance of her mind and the depth of her soul:

Harriet says, *"Oh, Child, I've always been underestimated, and I surprise folks all the time. It's my dark skin, my small size, and my woman's body that make people misjudge me. A Black woman born a slave who can't read or write does not fit most people's ideas of a great teacher. It's time for everybody to abandon their prejudices because a prophet can appear in any form at any time, even as the most neglected, overlooked, and forgotten among us."*

Harriet says, *"Child, the Underground Railroad was a secret society, and I've been the fiercest protector of those secrets till now. But now the time has come to open the archives so that you and others can understand. There are levels—stages—and much deeper meanings behind the Underground Railroad. Let's start with the archives."*

Deep within the vaults of the Underground Railroad live the archives—the preserved historical documents, testimonies, and eyewitness reports chronicling the life stories of Harriet Tubman and thousands of other ex-slaves. Not only do these archives provide a glimpse into the past, but they also affect the present. Since her physical death in 1913, Harriet's Underground files have grown considerably as more facts and information about her life continue to surface in a steady and mysterious flow. Just recently they found her father Ben Ross's home and even one of his hand-carved pipes. Everything from movies to books, quotes, documents, and even old photos is appearing now. These files remind me of *termas*, the Tibetan Buddhist term for hidden treasure or secret teachings. In Tibet, Buddhist masters would hide certain teachings and practices for a future generation to discover. Sometime these teachings would lie in waiting for hundreds of years, until just the right moment, and then would appear in consciousness. When our minds are ready, teachings and the teachers magically appear.

Harriet says, *"Child, I have many files and papers in the historical Underground archives, and these are very important to me. While I was alive, my papers were always mixed up, lost, and out of order. It bothered me to no end, and it feels good that all these records are finally being set straight. I appreciate all the folks working on this. It's important for the future generations.*

*"Then, Child, there are other files and archives about me and the Underground that you haven't seen; few people have. They're stored in 'nonphysical,' unearthly locations—in the air, the sky, in space, and within the mind stream in higher dimensions of consciousness. Some are in the spirit world. These other archives will be hard for some to believe. They chronicle my activities long before taking birth as a slave on a Maryland plantation."*

Suddenly, she begins moving quickly, showing me visual images and explaining how and where her historical and spirit files are archived. I see gigantic libraries in space—thousands of miles high with enormous file cabinets and stacks of documents. Then I see the Smithsonian Institution in Washington, D.C., where her historical documents are preserved in carefully marked zip-lock bags. I see small museums, libraries, and universities throughout the United States, where portions of her records and copies of documents are kept. We're flying through past, present, and future at the same time. These records are not static or fixed. Quite the opposite, they're alive and fluid, constantly in motion. Everything we do in the present affects the past and the future. Harriet is passionate about this topic and her explanation is like the Akashic records, often described as a vibrational record of every soul and its journey throughout space and time. Her explanations are also like teachings on karma, where our actions—both good and bad—are recorded and follow us from one life to the next.

Harriet says, *"Child, many great spirits, teachers, and powerful ancestors are opening their archives too. The whole spirit world has been flipped upside down, as millions of files that were once stored away, even hidden, are being made available."*

Harriet explains that everything, including all the inner Underground Railroad files, are being released directly into the collective consciousness, where they can be accessed through the mind stream. It's a direct trans- mission of teachings being spread, and it's accessible for all those who are ready. Harriet says, *"Child, the time is now and the dynamic energy operating the Underground is moving forward quickly. Most folks have fixed views about the spirit world and consciousness. I must encourage everybody to keep an open mind. There's so much more at work than what folks can understand right now. Child, there are different levels and stages to the Underground Railroad."*

On the outer level, the historical Underground Rail- road was a secret passageway—concealed, hidden from view. It was the unseen corridor where enslaved human beings passed through on disguised routes. The symbol- ism, profundity, and archetypal meaning surrounding the Underground is relevant for this moment in time. This invisible footpath that secretly carried countless unde- tected passengers along the road to freedom has both inner and outer meanings.

According to Harriet, her escape from bondage and her role as a conductor were part of an outer journey. The actual historical Underground Railroad with all its stops exists in the third dimension of our form-based reality. This is the earth level of density, solidity, physical matter, and form. It's everything we can touch with our hands and see with our eyes. If you look around you, it's this level of reality you'll see—our physical bodies, the furni- ture in our homes, our cars, and airplanes. Most of us live only within this dense world of form. Harriet calls it the "outer level." The problem is when we believe that this outer level is all there is. Harriet is saying there's much more to the story here.

Harriet says, "*Enslaved people had to live mostly on the outer level, because we were physically in bondage. I was able to lead many to physical freedom, but then they had to deal with their minds. They accomplished the first step, to be free to live and choose, but that left them with half the story. It was half the journey. They were free but not free. There are other steps, and we're at that stage in our understanding now, where many folks realize it's not just physical freedom that liberates us from bondage. It's the mind now that must be released.*"

If we live and exist solely on the outer level of reality, everything is dense, painful, and ultimately unsatisfying. We're like prisoners let loose; we can move all around, yet we still aren't free. We stay in bondage if we only live in the world of form and matter. The more we look at consciousness itself, the more we examine our minds directly, things get lighter and lighter. The first level of understanding is when we stop looking outward—and slowly, little by little, choose to look inward. Not everyone is ready for this level, but now there is a critical mass of people who are.

Harriet says, "*Oh, Child, there's another Underground Railroad that operates through the mind and moves through consciousness. This is the inner level, and it's always been kept secret until folks were ready and could understand. This inner spirit Underground Railroad is very much alive and operates exactly the same as the historical railroad. The inner railroad runs on light, wind, air, and thought vibration. There are conductors, station agents, supporters, organizers, and of course passengers. The routes are also long, strenuous, and filled with challenges and obstacles. We need the same strong determination to walk through the wilderness and scale high peaks, but now it's an inner journey. The Underground Railroad operates in parallel realities. Some folks are moving through the outer railroad and others the inner one. These are stages*"

*of understanding, and the outer and inner journeys are distin-*
*guished by levels of awareness. It's the same battle for freedom*
*and liberation, just one path is on the earthly physical level and*
*the other is in the mind, connected to sky, air, and spirit."*

Harriet says, *"When slaves escaped from the plantations*
*in Maryland looking for freedom, they escaped to the Northern*
*cities of Pennsylvania, New York, and Canada. For me and so*
*many of the passengers I conducted, these places represented the*
*Promised Land. Child, our vision of the Promised Land while*
*traveling on the Underground was a beautiful place where you*
*could finally stop and take a long rest. Freed from bondage,*
*without pain or suffering, you arrived in a heavenly realm filled*
*with peace and joy, and surrounded by God's love. This vision*
*kept our people moving forward. When folks wanted to give up*
*or they got tired on the Underground, it was my job to remind*
*them that a heavenly place awaited them."*

The term *Promised Land* was spoken by many in biblical times, during American slavery, and during the civil
rights movement in the United States. In his last speech,
given the night before he was assassinated, Dr. Martin
Luther King Jr. said, "I've been to the mountaintop. . . .
I've seen the Promised Land," adding, "I may not get there
with you. But I want you to know tonight, that we, as a
people, will get to the Promised Land." Dr. King's choice of
words on his last day on earth carries a timeless message,
and one for this moment in time. Barack Obama, America's first Black president, titled his presidential memoir *A*
*Promised Land*, also invoking this message of our collective
journey toward freedom.

Harriet says, *"Child, the Promised Land is not somewhere*
*outside. It's not an outer destination. It's inside each of us. The*
*Promised Land is a state of mind. It was promised and it's here,*
*but we must enter the inner Underground Railroad to reach it,*

to 'realize' it. *In the inner dimension, it's a symbol for complete freedom. Child, when I was born in 1822, I could only work on the outer levels. I helped people reach the outer level of the Promised Land, which they desperately needed. It wasn't the time for the inner level, so I kept quiet about it and did the work I needed to do.*

"*I didn't invent the inner Underground Railroad. It's a spirit that's been there for forever. Child, there have been thousands of conductors, station agents, helpers, and guides throughout time and space, in the form of light and energy. That's why I say I'm still conducting on the Underground. I'm still leading groups of passengers, and our destination is always the Promised Land.*"

Suddenly I hear myself yelling, "Wait, Harriet! Time out!"

Harriet and I have been in a long session. She had directed me to go to a remote cabin, saying that was what was required of me. So, I've been in this off-the-grid cabin in the Sierra Nevada, and I only stop our writing sessions to eat, take walks, and sleep. I've been on an emotional roller coaster for days, and I don't understand why. I can't stop crying between sessions, and I feel so much resistance to the whole process, especially this series of conversations, this chapter, which is surprising because I believe in everything she's saying. *Or do I?* The closer I get to Harriet—her energy and her words—the more pain I feel in my body. So, I call for a time-out and ask Harriet what's happening.

Even before she responds, I begin to realize that she is touching all the places inside me that are resisting what she's saying, and it's painful—physically and emotionally. It's like she's tuning a guitar that's way off pitch, and the more she plucks the strings, the more I want to scream and run away.

She's like a shamanic surgeon cutting away things inside me that are stuck. Did I think this book was going to be some fairy tale about channeling Harriet Tubman? I guess I must have, but there's no way she's ever going to let me get away with it. This is Harriet Tubman! I've got to be real, to have skin in the game. She wants it all—blood, sweat, tears . . . and love!

I watch her once-sweet grandmotherly expression turn wrathful. In a slow, stern voice, Harriet says, *"Child, what's wrong is that you've given up! You've stopped moving forward! I'm the conductor, we're on the Underground, and you're giving up!"* She says it over and over, and I realize it's true. I am giving up. I *feel* what she's saying, and this is why the writing and the talking have suddenly become so triggering and painful. I want to stop, turn around, and go home, by which I mean go unconscious.

Oh no! I have evoked the ferocious black panther that comes out when she's conducting and it's staring directly into my eyes. Harriet says, *"Who you tryin' to fool? Stop pretending, Springy!"* She sees the stuck place in me that always wants to stop, to quit when things get too hard, when the painful places of trauma within me get touched. Somewhere inside, I both trust and don't trust what she's saying, and I feel lost, like one of her passengers who wants to quit and go back to the plantation. *Why?* I wonder.

I begin to feel my heart, my body, searching for the resistance. *Where is it?* I ask myself. I just returned from Peru after leading retreats for seven months, taking a break from writing this book and from my sessions with Harriet. Peru is usually my power spot, where I renew my strength and my magic and connect deeply with the rain forest. This time Peru was different. I can only describe it as tragic. Two months into my time there, I fell down some stairs onto a glass pitcher that broke and cut my leg down to the bone. Eighty stitches later, I was released from the hospital and couldn't walk for weeks.

Then I was bitten by a sandfly and contracted leishmaniasis, a flesh-eating jungle disease. The treatment was grueling, 20 days of painful injections like chemo, and I had a terrible reaction. My hair began falling out, I was in agonizing pain, and I had to stay in bed most days. I felt like I was dying. At the same time, close relationships began falling apart and I had to fire a staff member I adored for sexual misconduct. The dramas were piling up, and life was taking its toll.

I begin to recognize that it's even deeper than Harriet pushing me and deeper than the traumas of Peru. When did I stop believing that freedom was possible? When did I give up on my aspiration for awakening? Harriet tells me I no longer practice what I preach. She says that I mouth all the right words, but my heart isn't in it anymore. And she's right. It's my self-doubt. It's consuming me.

Harriet says, *"I've seen this many times on the plantation—folks praying to leave, but when the time comes, they stay. They don't believe they can do it, and they give up."*

The next few hours are a blur of tears, throbbing head pain, heart palpitations, and some deep and profound insights. I see my father sitting in his car parked alongside the road or in a grocery store parking lot staring out the window talking to himself. He has given up on love. He refuses to see me even after I fly across the country to visit him. He has given up on me and on all his children. He has given up on life. I see my mother, who has been in an abusive relationship since I was 13. I haven't been able to visit her for years. The last time I tried, her husband unleashed his demons, and it took me years to recover. My mother has wanted to leave him many times, but then she tells me it's too hard and it's been too many years. I think about my grandmother Arlynn, who died by suicide. Out of the blue (or so it seemed), she hooked a hose up to her car exhaust in the back of a parking lot, turned on the car engine, and never woke up. A brother bound for the NBA became a drug addict. Another brother is in jail for repeating the same crimes over and over. The list of family members giving up on life goes on and on. No matter how hard I pray or love them or try to encourage them, I can't break through. At certain times, they all had a strong urge for freedom, and somehow, they all gave up. Harriet found that place in me—a seed deep inside me that also wants to give up.

Harriet envelops me in compassion. The panther is there, but now I'm her cub, and she's softer. She says, *"Child, I understand. You've been at this for a very long time."*

"Harriet," I say, still crying, "I don't remember a time in my life when I wasn't thinking about freedom and liberation. It has consumed all my attention, and it's the only real motivation I have in this life. I was born like this, my deep longing for freedom was never just for myself but for my family and everyone around me. I don't want to give up and I don't want to turn back, but I feel stuck."

Harriet says, *"Child, yes, the seed of giving up is there, and I know you can overcome it. We all must fight this battle within ourselves. Child, you must till the soil until you unearth a deeper level of faith, not blind faith but the kind of faith that's unshakable and unmovable. I know you have what it takes, but you must believe it too. You must believe in yourself, and if you truly want liberation, you need to see that it's in your own hands."*

Harriet says, *"Child, to enter the inner Underground Railroad, you must first want it, then be prepared to face all the obstacles that come up. You must always keep going. I'm trying to take you there, to show you that the chains you need to break are the ones inside. I'm your guide, your teacher, and your conductor. If you dedicate yourself to getting there, if you make a commitment that you'll never give up, Child, you will succeed."*

After what felt like a lifetime passed, and after a successful operation on my soul, the huge block between us evaporated. Everything feels so much lighter. I'm back on the inner Underground, and Harriet is right, there's no turning around now. I want to be free—not just for myself but for the benefit of all beings everywhere. I have to laugh at the intensity of it all. My sense is that Harriet is used to these types of breakdowns among her passengers. I spend hours thinking about the inner Underground and Harriet's faith in me. She is rescuing me again and her faith in me is like a huge gust of wind in my sails. I bow in wonder and gratitude for her magical presence in my life. I thank God. It's been an incredibly long day, yet something in me really wants to continue.

Harriet says, *"Good, Child, yes. Let's keep going."*

# Chapter 8

ıııııııııııııııııııım

# MOSES
# RISES AGAIN

I've spent most of my life immersed in studying and teaching Buddhist-based philosophy, but since meeting Harriet a deep longing for the Southern Black church has been rising in me. Listening to Mahalia Jackson and other gospel singers, I'm reminded about Harriet's lifelong devotion to God and the church.

I was about five when a family friend came to visit us for a few days, a very sweet woman who always smiled, and whose demeanor was very kind and gentle. Toward the end of her stay, she said she had a gift that she would like to give me. She had recently become a born-again Christian, and as we went into my bedroom, she handed me a beautifully designed children's Bible. Then she began flipping through the pages to show me the colorful illustrations, all the while talking about Jesus and God, and how much I was loved. The more she shared, the more excited I became. She kissed my cheek and we hugged at the end of our conversation. It was obvious to both of us how delighted I was with my magical new book.

I ran downstairs, Bible in hand, to share my excitement with my mother, who was standing in the kitchen. Within a minute, her face turned into a deep scowl and she snatched the book out of my hands. She stormed into the living room, and I could hear adults arguing. My mother was terribly angry, and I didn't understand why. When she finally returned, still frowning, my new book was gone. She told me in a firm voice to forget every word I had just heard and never to talk about it again.

I remained silent about the book and the topic of God's love for the next eight years. When I turned 13, I was introduced to Glide Memorial Church in San Francisco. My mother had heard about the church, and she thought I might like it. Maybe she felt guilty about snatching my children's Bible, I don't know, but after I got in trouble for shoplifting, she began taking me there regularly. I spent a couple of months paying off my community service working in their kitchen. The music, the stories, the people, and the energy are something I dearly miss. I loved it there and I remember feeling sad every Sunday when the services ended, my work was done, and I had to go home. My time there awakened something so deep in me.

I remember listening to Rev. Cecil Williams preach and I felt the presence of God's love in my heart—in his words, in the congregation, and in the church itself. It was so real. While he was preaching, oceans of "Amens," "Yes, Revs," and "Ummmm-hmms" would float through the air and out the windows. The choir was legendary, and the music brought everyone straight to their feet. I clapped, I danced, I sang, and then I cried. I felt so uplifted, and it had something to do with being a Black child. In that field of love with all those other brown faces, I felt good, even proud, about being a Black person for the first time. An unconscious wall of shame I didn't even know existed completely crumbled. Glide Memorial Church was in the Tenderloin district and the church pews were full of former addicts, prostitutes, homeless families, AIDS patients, gangsters, older Black women with glorious hats, gay couples, and me sitting in the front row. I remember thinking we were all so beautiful, and without a doubt, we were deeply loved.

As I got older, I began to believe that there was no place for me in the church anymore. I had become a Bohemian, my curly hair was tangled, my Indian shirts were wrinkled, and my unshaven legs and organic granola had, somehow, made me a misfit. So, after I found Buddhism I entered a long period of self-imposed exile, believing that I didn't need the church. Harriet laughs when I say these things out loud and tells me not to give up on it quite yet, that there may be something important for me to rediscover there. It feels significant to Harriet, and to me, that I remember the magic, the beauty, and the healing power within the Black church.

To honor and appreciate the spirit of Harriet Tubman and really catch the thread of her message, I realized I needed to reconnect with our Black roots and to her favorite biblical story about Moses from the second book of the Bible, the Book of Exodus. I only knew bits and pieces of the story, but with Harriet's encouragement I was inspired to learn more.

Harriet says, *"Child, there was an ongoing debate in the Southern white community whether to teach enslaved people Bible verses—especially the story of Moses, who was called by God to lead the Israelites out of slavery. The sad irony is hard to ignore, devout Christian slave owners debating whether to allow the story of Moses to be shared among those they kept in slavery. Child, they were afraid that these stories might inspire thoughts of freedom in us, and they did. Since it was illegal for enslaved people to read, they were passed down orally, and on Sunday evenings we would gather in the slave quarters, eat warm bread, and talk about Moses. Child, I can't tell you how much these stories meant to me; they were my only source of light in my darkest hours."*

Moses was the most important Jewish prophet and an important prophet in Christianity, Islam, Bahá'í, and other Abrahamic religious streams as well. He was an Israelite born in Egypt at a time when thousands of Israelites were being brutally enslaved. The Israelites were a small minority, but when the Egyptian pharaoh became aware that their population was growing, he commanded that every newborn Israelite boy be drowned in the river Nile. In a desperate attempt to save Moses's life, his mother left him in a woven basket among the riverbank reeds, where he was discovered by the pharaoh's daughter. Delighted and enchanted with this beautiful baby, she took him home and he was raised as a prince in the Egyptian royal family.

When Moses grew into adulthood, he saw an Egyptian slave master beating a slave, and Moses killed him. After that, he ran away from the royal family, and while alone on a mountain he encountered an angel and received a heavenly prophecy that it was he who would liberate the Israelites from bondage in Egypt.

He tried to negotiate with the pharaoh to free the slaves, but every time the pharaoh adamantly refused. After each refusal, God unleashed a series of terrifying plagues upon the Egyptian people and their land. Eventually, after tremendous suffering and destruction, the pharaoh agreed to release the slaves, and Moses led them all on foot out of Egypt. In one last-ditch effort to stop them from leaving, the pharaoh sent his army to kill them all. In a miraculous event, according to the story, God parted the Red Sea, allowing the Israelites to cross safely to the other side, then filling the sea with water again as the pharaoh's army chased after them, and the pharaoh's men all died.

After that, Moses and the Israelites embarked on a 40-year journey through the desert to reach the Holy Land. Harriet always saw her people as Israelites enslaved in the land of Egypt, and she herself embodied the spirit of Moses.

Some prophets are clairvoyant intermediaries who deliver teachings and messages from a divine source. Like Moses, Harriet too was a telepathic go-between, endowed with the ability to speak directly to God. And both Moses and Harriet found the inner strength to accept the heroic task of freeing their people.

Harriet says, "*Child, my dreams, visions, and conversations with God seemed to foretell a similar prophesy about my own life. I, too, saw the Promised Land, and I saw myself helping deliver my people there. I could see the future, and I could see the exact time when my people would, at last, be free.*

Is Harriet an emanation of Moses, a prophet, a saint, an angel, an awakened being? The question about who Harriet truly is has been on my mind since she first entered my life. Some still believe she was just a slave woman who got hit on the head and had some visions, but I know there is much more to this story. "Please, Harriet, tell me, who are you?" I ask. After repeating the question many times, she finally answers during one of our most powerful sessions, an extraordinary experience that lasted for several days.

Harriet says, "*Yes, Child. These are important matters, and I aim to answer all your questions about who I am and why I'm back. I am the runaway slave Harriet Tubman that history remembers, yet my spirit is far bigger than that. It's far beyond all labels, identities, and beliefs folks hold on to. Child, I've been called Moses for many lifetimes.*"

Harriet says, "*Child, I am a spirit now and my home is all of creation, the whole galaxy, and that's where I live and work. And my job is still the Underground Railroad—here in* the spirit world. I'm a track monitor, and my job is to supervise the conductors, trains, routes, and most especially the tracks themselves. I watch, check, and fix them whenever they're broken, and I help clear them when they're blocked.

"Everything up here runs like a giant railroad station but much faster and with much larger groups of passengers. Child, the universe is a big place. When I was alive on earth, my groups on the Underground were between 10 and 15 folks at a time. Here it's hundreds of thousands at a time. My task is to always keep the tracks clear and make sure the trains are running in the right directions.

"I can't say when I started this job, because I don't remember ever doing anything else. Child, it's been thousands and thousands of years. Many other powerful spirits here are also track watchers, inspectors, and monitors, and we work together. When a track becomes blocked, I'm notified because it can quickly turn dangerous. Millions could collide when a train goes off the track.

"Child, there are also runaway trains, which are a bigger problem because they involve both tracks and conductors. When there's a runaway train, we must take over as conductor so we can get it going in the right direction again. Every day I monitor stations and conductors and keep a close eye on every track. It's a big job, Child, and serious business.

"If for some reason we're not able to fix the problems from here, then we must 'go down' and try to fix it where it's broken. One of us must take on that task. It's a big assignment to get a train back on track from ground level, which usually means the earth level in the human realm. I've lived countless lives in many different places. Child, I always go where I'm needed the most; that's my job.

"That's why I chose to take birth as Araminta Ross on that plantation on the Eastern Shore of Maryland. I came for *a specific mission—to fix the track where it was blocked and broken. The people were desperately calling out for help, and my heart brought me there. It was my time to go, Child, and I took on the assignment knowing how difficult and painful it would be."*

Harriet Tubman appeared at a critical moment in history when the leaders of the United States were attempting to expand the institution of slavery into all the new territories they were acquiring. While other countries were abolishing slavery, America was considering turning the whole country into a slave empire. This was the runaway train heading in the wrong direction. It was perilously off track, especially for the 4 million enslaved people bound in chains and down on their knees crying out for help. Their prayers are what brought Harriet here in 1822.

Harriet says, *"Oh, Child, I could see the train was heading in a terrible direction. Slavery is a crime against humanity, and it destroys generations of people involved in it. We could hear their heartfelt prayers calling out for Moses and pleading for deliverance. They were suffering just as the Israelites were suffering in the land of Egypt. My heart was breaking and their collective cries for justice shook the gates of heaven open and down I came, Child, I arrived with the spirit of Moses in me because that's what the people needed. Some say I'm an emanation of him, and indeed I have been called Moses. But it's more like a reflection of the moon on the water or a spark that jumps out from a roaring fire. I am neither the moon nor the fire, just the spark, the reflection."*

Harriet Tubman was summoned from the spirit world as an answer to people's prayers. Instinctively, out of compassion for the suffering of humanity, she committed herself to assisting however she could, and as part of that commitment, she volunteered to "go down" and take birth in this world, then return at a predetermined time.

Harriet says, *"Child, many of us appear as prophets, saints, activists, clergy, and spiritual leaders. At other times, we appear as the poorest, weakest, and most hated. We take on different forms. We shape-shift according to the mission. We can appear as any gender, faith, or ethnicity, even as a child. I chose to be born as an enslaved Black woman to do my work, because that was what was needed to fulfill the task at that moment in time."*

Harriet's main mission was to help free the millions of Black people who were enslaved and to get slavery completely abolished in America, and she did it!

Harriet says, *"Child, I worked day and night getting this track straightened out. I was conducting on the outer Underground during the day and on the spirit Underground at night. Every time I fell into trance, I was traveling and working in the spirit world—receiving messages and getting the support and guidance I needed for how to fix the track. It felt like every angel in heaven showed up to help me get hold of that runaway train before it crashed. We all worked together, Child, to fix it here on the ground."*

Like Harriet, many of these great spirits have supernatural powers cultivated over countless lifetimes and missions. It's rare for them to display these powers openly, but they can bend time and space to fulfill their tasks when they need to. As in the biblical story of Moses parting the Red Sea, miracles and magic are often associated with these great spirits, especially in moments of crisis. The archetype I'm talking about here is that of a spiritual hero, an angel willing to walk into hell to help others. In the Buddhist tradition, this archetype is called a *bodhisattva*, an "awakening being." Sadly, some of these spirits, when they come to earth, are abused, tormented, or imprisoned. Their willingness to undergo tremendous hardship is a common theme in many of their lives. Their compassionate hearts allow them to face suffering and endure great hardships with wisdom, clarity, and resilience. They are fearless *protectors* who show others the way forward at times when all seems lost.

Harriet says there are many others like her who signed soul contracts "to go down" with specific missions to fulfill. Nelson Mandela, who left prison after 27 years to go forward and lead South Africa through the death of apartheid and the rebirth of his country, is one. His forgiveness and compassion were the lamps he carried during that dark time. His Holiness the Dalai Lama said he took birth intentionally to lead his people during the horrific destruction of Tibet and the genocide of his culture and millions of his people. Dr. King was born to lead thousands of people across the Edmund Pettus Bridge in Selma, Alabama, to get the civil rights bill passed and to lead the great March on Washington in a movement toward freedom and change. These beings arrive with a clear mission to complete, and when their piece of the mission is done, they move on to their next task.

Harriet tells me she has lived countless lives and now has the power to choose when and where she will take birth. She has reached a level of freedom where she can do that. She goes where she's needed the most, often appearing during times of war and genocide, struggle, and social change. She comes when oppressive systems are near collapse and *great shifts* are underway, as we are experiencing in this moment in time. In the Buddhist tradition, great beings like Harriet Tubman, Nelson Mandela, Thich Nhat Hanh, and Dr. King are seen as bodhisattvas, or enlightened heroes. Bodhisattvas cultivate the mind of awakening and make a vow to be of benefit to all beings. An 8th-century Buddhist monk, Shantideva, wrote this prayer, which is at the heart of the bodhisattva vow:

*May I be a guard for those who need protection,
a guide for those on the path, a boat, a raft, a bridge
for those who wish to cross the flood. May I be a lamp in
the darkness, a resting place for the weary, a healing medicine
for all who are sick, a vase of plenty, a tree of miracles. And
for the boundless multitudes of living beings, may I bring
substance and awakening, enduring like the earth and the sky
until all beings are freed from sorrow and all are awakened.*

Vows are aspirations, intentions we hold in our consciousness, noble seeds of love planted in the ground of our hearts. In every spiritual tradition, this quality of compassion is cherished. It's the ache we feel in our hearts when we encounter someone in distress. It's not pity, it's *care*, and it comes with a heartfelt wish to help. You don't need to believe in rebirth or spirits to appreciate Harriet Tubman's selfless compassion. Her very being inspires us, and some of us may choose to follow her teachings as a spiritual path.

Harriet says, *"Everything I did, Child, was for the benefit of others. This is an essential quality for conductors and those helping on the Underground. It's important that folks understand how deep this goes. Child, I was called by a higher power to roll up my sleeves and engage directly. I didn't just wish and pray for others, I moved forward to help relieve the pain of those around me. I am not free until all are free—this is a powerful statement, a Declaration of Compassion. To care deeply about the suffering of others can awaken the desire to act."*

I ask, "Harriet, were all your heroic actions, including your mission here, driven by this heartfelt desire to free others?"

Harriet says, *"Yes, Child. Real compassion destroys selfishness and mind games. Compassion enters the suffering directly, seeking to end it. It's free and it's fearless. It's love and wise action expressing themselves, working to alleviate pain like a river flowing. That's its nature."*

I ask, "How does it work? Do you feel it in your mind? Do you feel it in your body?"

Harriet says, *"Child, it animates my spirit with a pure motivation, and when compassion builds in me, my body, speech, and mind become extensions of it. I become the vehicle for it to express itself. This is a powerful form of love, and when it's turned toward the suffering aspects of others, it can become a dynamic combination of motivation and movement."*

I ask, "How do we access this?"

Harriet says, *"Child, the energy of great compassion is boundless, far greater than our mental prisons. It's the quality of the heart, and it's in all of us, but most people can't access it because it's buried so deep. Look inside, then cultivate a strong aspiration to ease the pain of others wherever you can. It builds slowly from there."*

In Buddhist mythology, there's a story that on one blessed occasion, all the Buddhas in all celestial realms came together and gave all their compassion to the great Bodhisattva Avalokiteshvara, who had made a vow to free all beings from greed, hatred, and delusion. His goal was to liberate every single being from suffering, to empty the hell realms, and to set everyone on the path to freedom. He worked tirelessly for an incalculable eon, giving everything he had to accomplish this mission. Then he stopped to assess his work. When he looked, he saw countless beings circling through the universe still trapped in delusion, still churning on the wheels of greed and hatred, and his heart broke. In that moment he was so overcome with grief, he exploded into a thousand pieces.

Just then, the Great Buddha of the Western world, Amitabha, appeared before Avalokiteshvara, and he and many other great beings lovingly put Avalokiteshvara's body back together again. But this time, instead of two arms, they gave him a thousand arms. And instead of two eyes, they gave him a thousand eyes, one in the palm of each hand so he could see the suffering of the world more quickly and powerfully and respond. Avalokiteshvara began weeping. Out of these tears of compassion, Tara appeared, an awakened Buddha in feminine form. She vowed to become Avalokiteshvara's devoted ally until his heroic task was completed. Moved by her vow, he recommitted to fulfilling his great vow, promising that he wouldn't stop until every single being is free.

Session after session, chapter after chapter, Harriet has been teaching and reminding me of aspects of myself I've overlooked, neglected, or disregarded entirely. She has begun to show me how the spirit of Moses is rising in me as my heart grapples with the issue of freedom and Black equality. What my white mother didn't understand is that when she took away my children's Bible out of fear, she innocently severed one of my roots. Part of my spiritual linage and strength is connected to Harriet Tubman, Martin Luther King Jr., Moses, and the Black church.

Harriet says, *"Child, there is a stream of liberation, great compassion, and spiritual power that flows down through the Black church. Many heroes, heroines, and great beings come through that stream. The movement for Black liberation started in the church, we organized in the church, we prayed in the church, and that stream now flows down through you."*

Something very powerful shifted in me during my sessions with Harriet in this chapter. She restored and renewed a part of my root system that had been damaged and severed. I made another vow that I would never give up on our ancestor's "dream" of a better world. If my task is to carry a piece of the movement forward, and to help build something new, then I humbly accept it. I too want a kinder world, a more loving world, a world in which justice and compassion include everyone. Through Harriet, you, me, and the spirited songs sung on Sunday mornings in Black churches, Moses is rising again.

---

## A Prayer

We give thanks to Harriet Tubman for her heart
and for giving us so much inspiration. We send love
and gratitude for all great beings who are working tirelessly for the benefit of all beings everywhere. We give
thanks to Moses, and I pray that the light of compassion
will awaken in each of us. We give thanks to all those
with loving, strong, compassionate hearts. We give
thanks for the Black church that has helped
our people stay strong for so long.

---

ıımıııııımıımıımıuuı

# GENERAL TUBMAN AND THE CIVIL WAR

Harriet says, *"Oh, Child, I had so many visions about this war long before it came. I felt it in my bones, and I smelled it in the air. Freedom is mighty sweet, and my people were going to taste it at last."*

Harriet chose to walk headfirst into the storm of the Civil War, and with the spirit of Moses illuminating her path, she blazed a trail that we're just beginning to recognize and understand. Harriet Tubman was the first woman in U.S. history to lead military raids. She was called General and she commanded her own troop of Black soldiers. She was also a gifted nurse who saved many lives. Harriet was a great war hero, and there's no doubt that her incredible feats and courageous deeds have been buried all this time primarily because she was Black and a woman. Most people are completely unaware that Harriet spent three long years as an enlisted Union soldier. Her great contributions to this country along with her military achievements have been left out of our history books. I must say, Harriet is very passionate about the topic of historical records and archives. It's been a core theme that she has brought up on many occasions, especially during our sessions about the Civil War.

Harriet says, *"Child, it's very important to fix the history books. A lot has either been left out or contains only half truths. As old details about my own military life surface, I hope it helps folks understand that white historians have written me and many others right out of history. This way of doing things needs to change, Child, it's just not right. All the records and archives must be sorted out and mended. This is of great importance to me; it's why I speak about it so often. It's on behalf of future generations, Child; they need to know what's true and what's not."*

Harriet's life is the personification of a heroine like Joan of Arc, who, when others gave up, refused to. Every battle fought and every obstacle overcome seemed only to make Harriet stronger. Her determination grew with each step in her unrelenting march toward her people's freedom. Through her years as a conductor on the Underground Railroad, all her supernatural abilities, her strategic mind, and her God-given gifts were molded to perfection. She became a skilled warrior, and when the first war shots were fired, Harriet Tubman began preparing herself to go into battle.

Harriet says, *"Child, I knew that the Good Lord was preparing me for something big. I foresaw everything I would go through from beginning to end. When the North and South declared war on each other, I knew what I had to do. I wanted to join the war effort because I knew I could help win it. I wasn't happy about the war at all; I just understood that it was necessary.*

*"It had to end, Child, the whole damn system of slavery had to end, and I was going help it end. I knew I could be of service, and I was, Child. I really did my part."*

The idea that the United States has ever been truly *united* is a figment of our collective imagination, a fantasy many of us are slowly giving up on. Black people really understand that America has always had two distinct sides with radically different ideas about what freedom and democracy are. We embrace ideas of diversity, inclusivity, and constitutional rights for everyone, while at the same time we simply don't live that way, and many don't even believe in it. If we look closely at American history, especially while the nation was being established, there were already enormous cracks in our country's foundation, a deep moral dilemma that goes back to the Founding Fathers. George Washington, the first president, owned more than 100 slaves, while Benjamin Franklin freed his slaves and became a devout abolitionist. Both these men helped write the Constitution, and this ideological crack concerning basic human rights was there from the beginning.

Harriet says, *"Child, if you build your house on a foundation of greed, hatred, and delusion, eventually it will collapse. It may a take a long time, but its collapse is inevitable. This is the law of universe, Child."* The United States built its entire house on the system of slave labor and the genocide of Native people. Slavery was a system of labor, power, politics, wealth, and the deeply embedded mindset of white supremacy. For the system of slavery to finally end and for constitutional rights to be extended to Black people, the United States itself had to collapse, and it did exactly that—from top to bottom—during the Civil War years.

James Baldwin wrote: "History is not the past. It is the present. We carry our history with us. We are our history. If we pretend otherwise, we are literally criminals." To understand the deep divisions and violence of today, we need to understand the violence of the past. The Southern states formed their own army to fight against what they called the "tyranny" of the Northern states and its ideas about abolishing slavery. Most Northerners wanted only to limit the spread of slavery, but many wanted it to end altogether. Thus, slavery and human rights were the focal points of the entire crisis. Four long, bloody years of Civil War with nearly three quarters of a million soldiers' deaths was the price of freeing millions of enslaved human beings and putting an end to the overt institutionalization of slavery in America.

Harriet says, *"Child, this was no small matter. The system of slavery was beginning to end, and folks had strong views about it. I saw families, friends, neighbors, even people who grew up together and went to the same church fighting and even killing each other over different beliefs. Child, it was an unavoidable war. The unjust system that America had built everything on had to go. It was time."*

John Albion Andrew, a prominent anti-slavery lawyer and wartime governor of Massachusetts, someone Harriet considered a friend, personally recruited her to join the war effort. Andrew helped create the celebrated all-Black 54th Massachusetts Volunteer Infantry Regiment, the first of its kind. Harriet's reputation as a conductor on the Underground Railroad as well as her knowledge of and familiarity with marshlands in the South made her an ideal spy. She would report directly to Colonels James Montgomery and Thomas Wentworth Higginson; both were abolitionists she'd known before the war.

While thinking and writing about the war chapter, I begin to notice that I have a removed and disconnected feeling. I'm in my cabin up in the Sierra Nevada. I built a big fire in the woodstove; there's still snow on the ground from the recent storm. I feel really tired and hesitant to begin another session. I'm sitting on a big brown leather couch. To cheer myself up, I begin imagining Harriet as a superhero. "Go, Harriet. Go," I chant, as if I'm holding pom-poms and cheerleading. The clock on my computer reads 12:30 P.M. when everything begins to change.

The high-pitched ringing starts, my heart begins racing, and my entire body begins shaking so much I can no longer hold my teacup. Harriet's face appears inches from mine with a very intense look. I haven't felt her this close since she visited me months earlier and gave me the book task.

It feels like she's going to slap me across the face, but instead she lowers her gaze to the area around my heart and then pushes her fist right through the center of my chest. I get extremely dizzy; nausea arises, and I can barely stand up. I head to the bed behind the couch and lie down flat on my back just as everything begins to intensify. I feel afraid—*Oh no, Harriet's mad I was being so silly*, I think. I feel as if I'm falling under the earth, under the water, and I begin to cry and pray. I'm trying to hold on to something with my hands, but everything is slipping through my fingers. I desperately want to call my teacher Jack Kornfield and tell him what's happening to me. *I need help! Please, Harriet, I feel suffocated.* The walls are closing in, and my body starts choking on pain and grief. Deep sobs are stuck in my chest, and they come out in noisy gasps accompanied by sounds of distress. I see Dr. King's face and beg for his help. I'm falling. I'm dying. *Harriet has finally killed me*, I think.

Then the overwhelming sensation of falling ends; it's like being in an elevator that finally stops. The doors open, and I see a large, open grassy field where hundreds of Black soldiers are sitting. The sun is shining, the sky is clear blue. It's another visual "memory," similar to when I had a glimpse of running on the Underground Railroad. Harriet is showing me something else; it feels different this time.

I'm stronger, my capacity has grown, and I can be present with the physical distress for much longer.

As I enter the scene, Harriet is in the distance sitting beneath a tree talking to the soldiers, who are in very neat rows facing her. I take in the scene while trying to hold myself together; the energy in my body feels so intense. Slowly, I begin walking toward her. She sees me, gestures for me to stop walking, and then speaks.

Harriet says, *"Child, this is very serious business. Please collect yourself and pay close attention. I would like to introduce you to your ancestors."*

As if on command, the men, in unison, turn around and face me. They are sitting and I'm standing. I am standing in a sea of men, rows and rows of men sitting perfectly still in full military dress. I look around and my eyes begin to meet their eyes. It feels like hours pass while I'm looking into their eyes in silence—sad eyes, scared eyes, tired eyes, bewildered eyes, lonely eyes, eyes briming with tears, eyes desperately fighting back tears. I look directly into the eyes of these brave Black men who have all seen far too much pain in their young lives.

Harriet then says in a gentle voice, *"Child, try hard to look deeper. Really see them, not just with your eyes."*

I continue looking. Now I take in their entire faces; then I begin to see underneath their uniforms. I see young bodies with deep scars, cuts, wounds, injuries from whips, ropes, and fists. I'm now standing up in my cabin walking in slow circles, holding my heart to help unlock all the tears that are stuck in my chest. I seem to be in two places at once, both in my cabin and there with Harriet.

As I look deeper and deeper, they begin talking as if by invisible command, a chorus of voices. My name is James; my name is Winston; my name is John; it goes on and on. I am from Mississippi; I am from Alabama; they tell me where they're from and how old they are. Some don't know their age and they tell me that as well. As I listen to their names, ages, and places of birth, I begin to *feel* them in my own body, not just see them. I close my eyes as hundreds of images begin flashing—the brutal beatings are there, but for me the emotional and mental abuse feel even worse, the inner wounds of the constant barrage of hatred, degradation, and humiliation. I hear the N-word over and over and it feels sickening. I see images of their mothers being sold, their fathers dying, their babies being taken from them, their exhausted bodies covered in dust hunched over in cotton fields. I straighten my back and stand upright, allowing my heart to open and let them in.

I'm weeping, and I hold my hands out in front on me, praying and singing an old Hebrew song to them. As I sing, my mind is flooded with beautiful images of their courage, love, and dignity. I see their acts of goodness, their kindness toward others, their virtue, wisdom shining out, their love for God, and I see their unwavering faith in Harriet Tubman. I see that despite everything that they've gone through, they're ready to fight for their freedom and their children's freedom too.

The sobs that have been stuck in my chest for hours are finally being released like small waterfalls, and the tears begin cascading down, soaking my face, neck, and the front of my sweater. Every cell of my being is full of love and compassion for these beautiful men. "I see you, Beautiful Ancestors, I see you!" I say it over and over as I hold my hands out to them, and I begin moving and touching and holding the hands of as many as I can.

As the scene finally fades away, I look at the time and it's 4:30 P.M. Four hours have gone by; I'm completely exhausted, and I feel moved beyond words. The scene fades but their eyes will be with me forever, I have no doubt about that. Harriet was so right: this is serious business.

Harriet says, *"Child, there is very little mention about all the Black soldiers who enlisted. Nearly 300,000 former slaves bravely fought not only to keep the Union together, but for their own freedom and dignity. The Union would never have won without them. I love those men, Child, they were so brave, and you need to understand how much their lives mattered. You also need to understand that they were a big part of the reason I chose to 'go down.' They needed my help, Child, this war was serious business, and I became Moses to help lead them so we could win this terrible war."*

Harriet says, *"Child, the year was 1861 and my assignment was to travel to Beaufort, South Carolina, cross enemy lines, and gather intelligence for the Union Army. My job was to establish a far-reaching spy network throughout the state. I was in familiar company, working under two brave commanders who were both abolitionists. I was ready to go, but my first assignment got delayed because I was desperately needed as a nurse at the camps in Virginia. War zones, Child, are truly hell; don't let anybody tell you otherwise. That was one of the toughest times of my life. I saw death and destruction everywhere I looked."*

Harriet arrived at the large Fort Monroe in Virginia, and there was also a tent city full of troops nearby. The encampment, the rations, and the outbreaks of disease were dreadful, and the number of soldiers grew every day. It became a magnet for escaped slaves seeking shelter from the escalating war, which presented its own set of struggles and hardships.

Harriet says, *"Child, the state of these makeshift hospitals was unbearable. I was at a loss for words when I arrived and* saw the horrid, unsanitary conditions. Truly, Child, the things I witnessed there were unspeakable. Whole regiments were dying of yellow fever, cholera, and dysentery. The intense heat mixed with blood, flies, feces, and dead bodies became breeding grounds for disease. Everyone was getting sick. As more and more wounded soldiers were brought in, we never had enough medicine or help, so I cared for hundreds of soldiers during that time. Many had been shot with cannons and guns, and their bodies were torn apart and full of holes. I saw doctors covered in blood while cutting off arms, legs, hands, and feet. My only focus was on saving as many lives as I could. I worked all day and stayed up most nights carefully washing bodies, wrapping wounds, and consoling the men who were praying to God while crying out in agony. Child, I held the hands of more dying men than I can count. I comforted them and prayed for each one with all my heart. They were so young, and many just wanted someone with them in their final hours.

"Slowly and steadily, I began to gain respect and influence among the men in and around the camp for my skills as a nurse and a healer. Every morning just before sunrise, I would head into the forest searching for plants to make my medicines. Child, I always had this knowledge, understanding, and love for plants; I knew which ones to pick and how to use them.

"During my years as a conductor on the Underground Railroad and even before that, I was an herbalist, a quality I liked about myself. I was able to treat anything with plants—from cuts and bruises to infections and serious illnesses. I would boil the plants down into strong teas, and these brews proved effective at treating dysentery, which was killing many soldiers. We often ran out of traditional medicines, and the doctors began to rely on my knowledge of plants and herbs. My skills and remedies were in high demand. I also spent a lot of time helping the

Black soldiers, who were dying at a rate four times higher than the white soldiers.

"Oh, Child, I fed and comforted many Black soldiers who were struggling to survive and did my best to encourage them and nurse them back to health. Because of my reputation as Moses the Liberator, I was very popular in the camp. They found peace in my presence, so I sang religious songs, and we prayed together every night. I gave them hope, dignity, and most of all faith that a much brighter future awaited them. I always tried to keep everyone in high spirits, so when I wasn't in the hospitals, I stayed up late into the night baking everyone ginger cakes and cooking whatever else I could find.

"Newly freed Black folks kept pouring into the camps, and they needed every kind of help and support imaginable. They'd left the plantations with nothing, and the world they were entering was being torn apart by war. I was there greeting everyone with open arms. I needed to be there for them, Child, and I taught them how to cook, sew, and organize, so they could become self-sufficient. I helped families locate relatives, move north, and find proper housing. I was constantly raising money through my Northern allies for clothes, food, and everything else these formerly enslaved people needed to survive. What started out as a short stay at Fort Monroe turned into a year and a half.

"Child, by early 1863, with the war raging all around us, I was ready for my next assignment—the one I'd been recruited for and had seen in my visions. I headed down to South Carolina and entered the belly of the beast directly, Child. It was swarming with enraged white Confederate soldiers and mobs of their armed supporters. I knew in my heart that my spirit was needed there, and I knew what to do to stay alive. I was constantly talking and gathering intelligence while I worked. I have to say I was a good spy, and I learned the details of the terrain and all the hideouts. Finally, I was authorized to form a team of *scouts to infiltrate and map out the interior of the upper South, and after that I began to plan strategic raids."*

During our sessions about this chapter, Harriet became very lively and energetic. She has so many war stories, I could fill a whole book with just those tales alone. I get the sense that she is so passionate about this time in her life because it's never talked about. We only talk about her as a conductor on the Underground or even a nurse in Virginia, but not as a military general.

One of Harriet's most successful military missions was the raid at the Combahee River Ferry in South Carolina. Maybe it was because she'd already had visions of the future that made her so utterly fearless, but regardless, I bow to her courage. If I had any lingering doubts before about Harriet Tubman being an emanation of Moses, this story took away all my uncertainties.

Harriet says, *"Child, I had planned this mission for a long time. I and 300 Black soldiers slowly sailed a large number of boats up the Combahee River in the dead of night. My mission was to cut off the supply line that supported the Confederate soldiers. I had also discovered through my spy network that many slaves had fled their plantations and were stuck in the middle of the battle zone. Many were being murdered and hunted down. Hundreds were stuck, lost, and hiding in the woods. My job was to rescue as many slaves as possible.*

*"Once we arrived at just the right spot, my men quietly jumped out of the boats and began to set fire to everything in sight, including rice fields, bridges, and buildings, just as we had planned. Enslaved men and women on their way to work saw the Union boats and ran toward them. Within a short period of time, hundreds began running toward us, some carrying their children in their arms and what little they owned on their backs. I stood on the upper deck and welcomed them*

*all until every boat was filled to capacity. They ran despite the efforts of overseers and Confederate soldiers shooting at them and forcefully trying to stop them. Child, they just kept coming and coming, and things were starting to get out of control. The boats became so full that panic began to take over, almost capsizing some of the boats.*

*"At that moment, I began to sing an old religious hymn I had learned from my mother. It had some kind of magical effect on the crowd, and they immediately calmed themselves and we were able to sail back up the river successfully without capsizing. Child, it was a massive undertaking, and a great victory. More than 750 slaves were rescued that day and the raid was a direct strike on the Confederate army. Child, when we all got back to camp, we had a big celebration. We sang and we laughed all day and even into the next night. My people didn't know what to think when they saw me gallantly dressed in my full uniform, sailing along, standing tall as the commander on that boat. I was always called General Moses by Black folks and Black Moses by the white officers. It was hard for the white generals and soldiers to believe that I had pulled off such a successful raid. They seemed to like having the Black Moses fighting alongside them. With so many soldiers dying, I became a powerful symbol of good luck. Child, I continued with my spy efforts and led other raids, helping the Union Army win victory after victory."*

Harriet's prophetic journey resembles the biblical story of David and Goliath. She too was beckoned to fight a battle that seemed impossible to win. In her case, it was the life-and-death struggle to fulfill her mission to eradicate the institution of slavery in America. I feel so proud that Harriet Tubman, along with more than a quarter of a million other Black soldiers, most of whom were formerly enslaved, accomplished the task. In April of 1865,

Confederate general Robert E. Lee finally surrendered, officially ending the war. The cost was enormous—the United States was practically bankrupt, President Lincoln was assassinated, and the South lay in ruins. It shows us how strong this "program" was and what it took for it to collapse. In the end, people were *forced* by new laws to stop brutally enslaving other human beings, though many never reached an enlightened view about it.

Harriet says, *"Child, you must always remember that love and truth are the most powerful forces in the universe, and they will never let you down. On the battlefield, I was never alone; I was always accompanied by celestial guardians and unseen forces. While I fought on the ground there, I was also engaged in a much bigger battle and that was in consciousness itself. I fought hard to end slavery, but my bigger goal was to eradicate the mindset behind it. Child, it was spiritual warfare, and many of us were fighting to put an end to the inhumane thinking that had brought about the creation of the brutal system of slavery. Child, believe me when I tell you that thousands upon thousands of spirits are constantly involved in ongoing wars to uproot greed, hatred, and delusion in the minds of men."*

Before starting this chapter, I spent a lot of time studying all I could about the Civil War and the periods before and after it. I read books, watched documentaries, and read blogs, and throughout it all I experienced tremendous amounts of grief and sorrow. History is humanity's road map of lessons, mistakes, and teachings. It took courage for me to face the truth about America's history; it's a long, pain-filled record of our collective evolution.

Harriet says, *"Child, I understand your grief, and as you and others learn to reconcile American history, it will be a big step forward for the planet. Awakening is an evolutionary process in which we arrive at the complete understanding that love is all there is. My job as a track monitor in the spirit world is to keep folks on trains that move them in this direction. I'm always battling to keep the trains on the right track, because there are always destructive energies attempting to derail the trains and push them in the directions of sorrow, hatred, and misery."*

These destructive energies manifest themselves as bullies and tyrants who create or perpetuate cruel systems of oppression. And there are always stories of great leaders, compassionate beings who try to guide us in the direction of kindness and wisdom. We all share these collective traumas, and we all share the redeeming qualities of love and freedom. According to Harriet we are both the tyrants *and* the heroes, and it's up to us to decide who we want to be. Ultimately, we each have free will—you see, this is a "choose your own adventure" experience and your life choices are heavily influenced by your mind.

In history there is one essential truth that seems to stand out beyond all others. One lesson that is highlighted again and again is our tendency to repeat painful mistakes over and over. In the Buddhist tradition they call this *Samsara*, the wheel of suffering or endless wandering in delusion. In ancient India, these mental habits were called *maya*, "illusory." In the West, it's considered a form of insanity. Fundamentally, it's the confused mind constantly looking for happiness while planting and replanting seeds of pain and suffering. It's so hard for us to accept that love is all there is.

Harriet says, *"Child, I am a warrior and I've fought in many battles over countless lifetimes, and it's always for love. Throughout my life and during the war, I wasn't fighting to hurt folks; it was the opposite. I'm a protector and my vows are always to protect and save lives. Child, most days I carried a loaded pistol because I had to, to get my job done, but I'm a sacred warrior and my heart is absolutely committed to nonviolence. I never attempted to take a life or even harm anyone. I had to pull my gun out many times, but it was just a part of the illusion. I looked fierce, but I never had a drop of hatred in my heart, just love, Child. I did everything out of love and compassion."*

Harriet tells me she wants people to understand that her fight was not just about abolishing slavery, but fighting for something good that she always felt was there about America. *"My fight to abolish slavery was a fight to abolish the consciousness of inhumanity. It goes deeper, much deeper. Child, don't ever give up on the dream of America, the dream of progress. I understand some folks wanting to give up—the history has dark times—but I encourage them not to. For a very long time I've been planting seeds, mountains of seeds right inside those pain-filled cracks in America's foundation. Now they're growing, and I see a new sun on the horizon. There's a good spirit in America, something beautiful, and it's rising. It's awakening and it's worth fighting for. That is why I fought so hard during the war, and it's why I'm back now. The story is not yet over, Child. Other chapters are coming, important chapters."*

Harriet Tubman is extremely patriotic even though she experienced so much injustice. I've always had mixed feelings about and a complicated relationship with America, because of our history. So, it was a big surprise during our sessions when Harriet expressed so many patriotic feelings. She encouraged me to embrace both my ancestry and my citizenship. I thought about John Lewis, Fannie Lou Hamer, James Baldwin, Martin Luther King Jr., Maya Angelou, and so many others—civil-rights leaders, poets, and Black writers, all of whom were critical thinkers yet also patriotic. Then I reflected on Barack and Michelle Obama's eight years in power and the truth that this country elected Barack president not once but twice. There is a "soul" in America and it's what Harriet Tubman, Dr. King, and so many other civil rights heroes keep fighting for.

America is a great mirror, a reflection of our own minds, which is where the real battle lines are drawn. It's getting better, but each generation still has work to do toward healing this artificial divide. We need to see that the only "crack" is in the consciousness of the people. Sometimes I wonder if it's even possible to reconcile these two parts of our divided house and really heal the fracture in our country's foundation, in our nation's consciousness. The talk about another American Civil War today is hard to ignore—my alarm bells are ringing; we seem to be going back in time. After so much work and progress by so many people, we're back here again. Our country is so full of contradictions, but deep in my heart, I know there's a higher teaching in this for all of us.

Harriet says over and over, *"Don't worry, Child, truth and justice will always win, I promise you that it's the law of the universe. I'm back because I see something good. You must have faith that something important is underway. It's much bigger than what folks can see in the history books."*

She starts to show me images of herself in her old military uniform journeying through the cosmos, and she isn't alone. All the spirits and allies of the Underground are with her; and they're standing not only for love but for truth and justice. Harriet's enormous faith, her belief and confidence in a higher power, give me huge hope and peace of mind. She's ready to take her place as the general again and join the battle for progress, collective awakening, and always human rights for every single human being.

## A Prayer

I pray our wisdom will shine through and the ancestors
will ground and surround us with their love, their light,
their wisdom, and their deep compassion. I pray to the
Angels and protectors in all directions to guide our way
as we take refuge in the heart of wisdom. I give thanks
to Harriet Tubman and all the unsung heroes and heroines who fought and died for justice during the Civil
War. I honor the all-Black 54th Massachusetts Volunteer
Infantry Regiment and all the Black soldiers whose
bravery, dignity, and sacrifices changed history.
I see you, I remember you, and I thank you.

## Chapter 10

ᴵᴵᴵᴵᴵᴵᴵᴵᴵᴵᴵᴵᴵᴵᴵᴵᴵᴵᴵᴵᴵᴵᴵᴵᴵᴵᴵᴵ

# UNDERGROUND ALLIES AND THE NEW ABOLITIONISTS

Harriet says, "*Child, the Underground Railroad, the civil rights era, Black Lives Matter, and my legacy are part of the ongoing Movement for Equality. It's not just politics, it's about human rights, the right to life, liberty, and the pursuit of happiness. We swim together or we sink together. This is not a call to violence; it's a call to peace. This is not a racist movement; it's a movement to end racism. This is not a movement to take away rights; it's a movement to ensure that everyone's rights are respected and upheld. This is not a movement to take over a country or create a race war; it's an effort to end the war on Black and brown people that has been going on for centuries. We want peace and love, but never at the expense of truth and justice. Recognizing our beauty, and everyone's beauty and equality, and reminding ourselves of this over and over is part of the work to end the cycles of suffering and bring us to a brighter day.*"

We're carrying the movement forward with a new generation and a new name but with the same important cause at hand. The United States has a traumatic racial history, and Harriet Tubman is back to help the Underground because the work is still unfinished. She has been here before, and she knows what's at stake. Harriet has very passionate views about allies, leaders, and the focus of the movement today. She keeps telling me over and over how vital it is to know *what* we're standing up for and why.

Harriet says, *"Child, when I finally arrived in Philadelphia, the City of Brotherly Love, my mind was blown wide open. It was the winter of 1849, and I began to see the world around me with new eyes. This Northern city was so different from the Maryland plantation where I grew up. Here was a bustling city with a large population of 'free' Black people. As I walked down the streets, I saw my folks dressed in fine clothing with stylish hats and shiny shoes. These people had swag; they greeted each other joyfully, hand-slapping and even fist-bumping. These caged birds knew how to sing, their joyful energy was palpable, and the neighborhoods were humming with life."*

The Underground Railroad has always had deep roots in Philadelphia, and these roots are still very alive today. It was the same neighborhoods where Harriet once walked that rose up victoriously in the 2020 U.S. election to help defeat a racist president. In the 1850s, the sweet smell of freedom permeated the air, and it did again in 2020. Harriet's visions led her to exactly the right place. This was in a hotbed of active resistance, and she was among her kind of people. In the North, she would meet many dedicated abolitionists and key leaders of the American Anti-Slavery Society, which was the Black Lives Matter of the 19th century. Harriet joined this growing movement of well-connected allies whose influence spread throughout Philadelphia, Boston, and even Maryland. Although she was a wanted fugitive, she attended their meetings and shared her story openly. In a short time, she learned the inner workings of this secretive network of influential people vehemently opposed to slavery and dedicated to supporting those who were escaping.

Harriet Tubman became a part of the worldwide anti-slavery movement, which culminated in the founding of the National Association for the Advancement of Colored People (NAACP) in 1909, four years before she died. Established in response to the ongoing violence against Black people, the NAACP continued to lead Black folks through the bloodiest years of the civil rights era. And now we have Black Lives Matter, which started in 2013, again in response to escalating violence against Black and brown people. My friends, although Harriet Tubman lived more than a century ago, judging by my visions and from what I experience in conversations with her, I know that she is deeply familiar with everything that's happening now.

Today we're seeing millions of people taking a stand yet again against a delusional old racist program of the mind. These liberation movements of consciousness have been rising for centuries. Black Lives Matter is a response not only to police brutality and suppressed opportunities, but to the legacies of colonization, slavery, and Jim Crow. The Jim Crow laws of the late 19th century are echoed in today's redlining, gerrymandering, and Black voter suppression. Black people are *still* seen as "less than." Instead of lynchings, we have police shootings and civilian vigilantes with guns committing hate crimes. Mass incarceration and for-profit prisons now legally enslave an entirely new generation of young men of color. The alt-right white nationalist movement is just a sleeker version of the KKK wearing suits instead of white hoods. The Southern Confederacy has risen from the dead—if it ever died at all.

I begin to feel the tears of frustration building. The more I write, the more stuck and angry I feel. I cuss and complain to Harriet, "I'm sick of this shit! How long is it going to continue?" I feel like throwing my computer across the room and I have the urge to break everything in sight. It's pure rage. I don't act it out; I just notice the intense thoughts and images of being on a rampage, destroying everything in sight with a large baseball bat. Then my tears really begin, and I let them flow. As a Black woman, I feel the fatigue from holding this collective wound. My bones feel tired, and I abruptly collapse onto my bed in utter exhaustion. "Harriet," I say, "I'm so fucking tired." I say it over and over, allowing myself to *feel* the rage and the deep tiredness that's taken over my entire body. Within moments, I feel Harriet's love surrounding me, her strong hands holding mine. I see her smiling at me with compassion in her eyes.

Harriet says, *"Oh, Child, I understand how you're feeling, Lord knows I do. Each of us has felt this way—so damn tired of it all! I'm here to help you, and everyone, not just hold this pain but heal it. This wound was inflicted over a long period of time, and it's going take a long time to heal. It was inflicted by large numbers of people, and it will take the same amount of people, maybe even more, to heal it. I'll try to help you understand. We will get through this together."*

I realize during our session how much I need Harriet to help me make sense of this ongoing pain. For me as a healer and a teacher, it feels critically important to be able to bring healing to racialized trauma in all its forms. Not just for myself, but for everyone affected by this. I want to move past this but it's hard to know how. When old traumatic wounds aren't healed, they fester and bleed out into the streets—sometimes as a protest and other times as explosions of hurt and pain.

The wheel of time never stops, and neither will this painful delusion until we understand how to transform it. It's time to tackle the problem head-on, it's not new. We've been here before. Our ancestors have been here before, and Harriet has been here. It's the intersection, the crossroads of truth and delusion, generosity and greed and love versus hatred. This is another turning point, and I pray, for humanity's sake, that we do not take the "wrong turn" again. It's time for new choices—individually and collectively, as a society, a nation, and a world community. The situation is urgent, and our hearts are being called to the reckoning that's pounding on the front door. Seeing clearly is essential. The stakes are high, with consequences that have great spiritual and societal impact on all of us.

Harriet says, *"If we work together, you and me and this new generation of abolitionists, we can heal these old, festering wounds and change the course of history. Our Underground allies will never stop; there are many dedicated spirits—from the other side—helping you all heal and move forward. You must all work together, Child, always together. It's much too big to hold alone."*

Harriet starts explaining the dedication and commitment needed if we want to stand with her and the Underground. Becoming an ally involves stages, time, and practice. It's a dance; you take a few steps forward and a few steps back. It takes increasing awareness and evolving consciousness to become more aware of white supremacy and the systemic oppression of our brothers and sisters of color. We begin by being clear that we don't know everything. Those who became devout abolitionists, those who supported the Underground Railroad, did not start out knowing everything. Abraham Lincoln's mind was changed as he learned from people like Frederick Douglass, Sojourner Truth, and William Lloyd Garrison. We must open ourselves to new ideas, to seeing what's going on around us and, more important, inside us.

Let's begin by meditating on the words *Black Lives Matter*. These words are so powerful, and if we allow them to do their work, they immediately expose the racialized programming within us. That's why some people simply cannot say these three words out loud. It's so telling that three words have stirred up so much violence and controversy in our society these days.

*BLACK LIVES MATTER.*

These three words are so perfect and complete. Seeing these three words and saying these three words out loud can invoke so much emotion, both collectively and as individuals. These three words can invoke fear, hatred, and outrage mixed with righteous indignation. We can feel it in our bodies and in our psyches. Or they can invoke a deep sense of wholeness, respect, truth, and worthiness. The absolute genius in these three words is that they immediately reveal ourselves to ourselves. It's checkmate on the old racist program, so really notice how you feel when you say it. Are you even able to say it? If not, ask yourself why. Be curious about that.

*Black Lives Matter* is like a Zen koan, an unanswerable question that forces us to think in an entirely new way. Every time I say these words, I break open something deep within my being.

I am discovering the great power in this simple statement of truth. BLACK LIVES MATTER. Every time I say these words, I am breaking open something very deep within my own being. I find pieces of this program inside myself like giant shards of glass lodged directly in my heart. As I pull each piece out with great tenderness, I feel a huge relief. You can do it too.

The program of white supremacy depends upon my belief in my own inferiority, that I don't matter. It depends on me hating myself and devaluing myself because of my brown skin. It depends on you hating me too. Its invisibility has kept it going, but now its construct has been brought into the light for questioning and examination. This inquiry goes very deep, with a depth that we discover only by saying the words and then sitting with the great mystery of what it reveals to us. Try to listen with your heart; it knows exactly what to do. It's deep medicine because we are breaking a powerful program that has been operating for hundreds of years.

To be an ally and abolitionist working for the Underground, we must become willing to dedicate a part of our life's work and our energy to *holding, tracking,* and *disrupting* as a way of bringing healing to the historical wounds caused by white supremacy, colonization, and the institution of slavery.

*Holding* means we face history honestly and look at what has happened to black-bodied people over the course of hundreds of years. It hurts because there's a painful wound still there. As allies, we open our hearts as wide as we possibly can, and we willingly hold a sliver of this pain ourselves. It's a collective wound and it resides deep in the earth's energy body. Since we're all connected to the earth's energy body, we all feel the effects of this wound in consciousness, but in very different ways. When the pain from this wound arises, people respond differently, some with rage, grief, violence, guilt, denial, shame, fragility, and terror, to name a few.

It's much bigger than what any one person can hold because of the sheer numbers of people involved. Millions upon millions of people, including multiple generations of our ancestors both Black and white, have been affected. If each of us takes one piece of it, we can start to digest it through our own individual bodies. Just by our willingness to feel and bring our compassionate presence to this pain, we will begin to metabolize and dissolve it. When we begin to do this the earth body will also recover from this wound. Thousands of people are now doing this work by holding classes, workshops, rituals, and retreats focused on healing the wounds of racism. Helping groups to safely feel, see, and understand this collective pain and then helping them release it is one of the most important jobs an ally can take on at this moment in time.

*Holding* doesn't mean grasping, and we must be aware of the difference. It's like holding the hand of someone in pain until the pain eases. *Holding* in this context means to make space, to open to it, to feel and to allow. Healing happens by placing our loving attention on areas that hurt. We make space energetically in our bodies, not to keep the pain but to let it go. In the future we will be working with energy and learning how to heal, metabolize, and move the collective suffering faster and faster on higher and higher levels.

*Tracking* involves a couple of steps. The first is a commitment to looking deeply into our own ancestry and family trees. If we have benefited from systemic racism through money, land, and privilege, we make reparations in the best way we know how. We can begin to repair, restore, and amend many of the things that our ancestors did. It's never too late to right a wrong; in fact, it's a part of the process of healing the collective wound. We also commit to tracking the systemic impacts of racism and white-supremacist ideologies. We stay vigilant and observe how systemic racism operates around us. When we're aware, we see clearly and are far less likely to operate unconsciously within it. It's a practice of staying awake and a commitment to being the eyes and ears of the Underground.

*Disrupting* means we commit ourselves to interrupting and nonviolently resisting all unjust systems, wherever and whenever possible. Historically, the Underground Railroad was a powerful partnership of people working together, a coalition that included white and Black people who shared the goal of Black freedom. Their civil disobedience not only disrupted prevailing tradition, but also subverted federal law. The Underground Railroad was rooted in defiance and resistance. The abolitionists stood their ground and refused to cooperate with a system that was cruel and unjust. On the outer level, it's taking a stand when we see this injustice in any form. We work actively to disrupt all internal and external systems of oppression when we can.

The Underground Railroad worked because its strong alliances included everyone. It was a network of free Blacks, Quakers, clergy, women, and elected officials. An *alliance* is a connection among people, groups, or nations for mutual benefit to achieve a common purpose. Members of an alliance are allies, and everyone has a critical role to play.

Harriet says, *"Child, when I was a conductor on the Underground, so many brave folks stood with me. They offered their homes, baked bread, knitted blankets, wrote letters, hosted meetings, raised money, pushed the government, and constantly spoke up. A thousand invisible hands helped the movement by working together, each offering loving support in the ways they could. We each have our part to play; every action is valuable and every contribution counts."*

True *allyship* is a process of building relationships based on consistency, accountability, and—most important— trust. To *ally* means to *work together*; we are partners who stand up for one another no matter what. The abolitionists protected each other, and we can too. We can learn how to do this. Remember, this is a lifetime project. When Harriet was escaping north for the first time, she found many white people more than willing to assist her. Seeing this required a huge shift inside her, a mental and moral adjustment for her to trust these newfound supporters who looked very much like those who not long before had been her oppressors. The support and encouragement she experienced in moving through these circles of new friends touched her deeply, and she was able to let it in.

Harriet says, *"Child, I'd never been around so many whites who didn't treat me like I wasn't human, I had to get used to it! I kept asking, 'Are you really going to help? Are you really going to be there?' I quickly discovered that these white abolitionists were ready to risk everything for justice and for me."*

In fact, it was a radical group of young white abolitionists who helped light the fire that helped burn down the house that slavery built in America. They stormed onto the scene in the early 1830s, ready for battle—launching attack after attack on the institution of slavery, especially in the South. They called for the immediate emancipation of all enslaved people and fought shoulder-to-shoulder with Harriet in her heyday. Many were persecuted and beaten, and some died alongside their enslaved brothers and sisters.

The name of one heroic man appears again and again in our history books and within the Underground archives. He came up during my sessions with Harriet on several occasions.

Harriet says, *"Oh, Child, Garrison was a true man of God and the good Lord watched over him every day. He was so brave, and I respected him deeply. I want folks to know who he was, so please, Child, share about him now and in the future please tell his story."*

His name was William Lloyd Garrison. He founded the American Anti-Slavery Society and his revolutionary newspaper, *The Liberator*, was very popular *and* attracted many other white abolitionists. Despite his young age, Garrison became a central figure, and other young reformers began to join him. He became a nationally known writer, speaker, and publisher, inspiring many individuals with his courage to speak out, and through him dozens of anti-slavery groups began forming. He recognized that as a white male, he could use his power in ways that others couldn't, and he elevated the voices of former slaves, free Blacks, and women too.

For those of us who are Black and brown, it is important to know that there were, and are, white people on the side of truth and justice. Remembering this can help us work together peacefully, because staying united will always make the movement stronger. These young abolitionists left a legacy for our white brothers and sisters who often feel ashamed of their racist, slave-owning ancestors. These abolitionists are all our ancestors—yours and mine—and to remember them is very important. This movement today is about healing, uniting, and finding our courage to stand up. I honor those who put their lives on the line for my Black ancestors.

While doing deep allyship and liberation work, expect to be challenged in every way. On the outer level you may have to weather many storms, attacks, setbacks, and even violence. No matter what happens, stay in your heart and make the vow to stay completely nonviolent and just keep moving forward. On the inner level the work will take each of us on our own personal healing journey. Expect to be changed by the work. While writing this chapter, painful memories of growing up biracial began to arise all over again. My father was a dark-skinned African American man, and my mother is white. Interracial couples were controversial in the late '60s, and my parents had a hard time finding a minister who would marry them. Finally, they were wed in a tiny Nevada chapel. But they were subjected to hatred and racism daily, and their marriage unraveled quickly. My father did not have the resources or support to deal with the traumas he experienced growing up as a poor, uneducated Black man in America. My mother's response was obliviousness, and after he left, she pretended that her children were white. I spent years feeling at war between these two sides within myself, just as America is at war with these two parts of itself. Each of us has a piece to hold, and it's going to be bigger than we can imagine.

Now is a unique moment in history, and we have a new generation of allies powerfully emerging with diverse skill sets, approaches, and methodologies. We have entered a new age where space, wind, and the air elements are dominant. This is where Harriet lives, conducting from her headquarters in the universe beyond time and space. Things move faster through air and light waves, so big change can happen in the blink of an eye. We are shifting into a much higher level of consciousness, and our 21st-century technologies reflect that.

We can spread our messages worldwide much faster and entire movements can happen in ways our ancestors could only dream about. We must remember to act responsibly as we take bold evolutionary leaps forward. We can use the Underground Railroad as a framework, adopt Martin Luther King Jr.'s strategies, and rely on our ancestors like Harriet to form a solid foundation for our work. The essentials never change, but they can be adapted and communicated in new ways to meet this moment in time. Finally, we must always stay united; we need to work together. We need one another, especially in this new movement rising today.

There are three levels of abolitionism: Inner, Outer, and Ultimate. *Inner abolitionism* is the dedication to our own personal liberation, it's our commitment to walking the path of the inner Underground Railroad. Our delusional programs of mind are not new; they have been well established by our ancestors and their ancestors before them. They live deep within our bodies, our neurocircuitry and our nervous systems. We get so much more than hair and eye color from our parents. We get all the stories about who we are and who we aren't, and many other ways of thinking that may no longer be compatible. You need a strong personal practice both spiritually and at times even psychologically. Awareness and mindfulness allow us to remain vigilant so we can see and feel these programs in real time. We can appreciate and honor the depths of our healthy roots and get the help, support, and resources we need to uproot the unhealthy ones. To be effective we must commit to constantly doing the ongoing work of abolishing our own internalized greed, hatred, and delusion.

*Outer abolitionism*, to be successful, must always stay rooted in love and wisdom. Sowing seeds of violence is both unproductive and counterproductive. It is critical that we practice active nonviolence, not passively standing by, but advocating in bold and creative new ways. Violence may break out around us, we may even get injured or arrested, but we must commit to staying nonviolent at all times. Working for freedom is a calling and a deep spiritual path. We become part of a living lineage of freedom fighters committed to liberation for all. Everything we do is based on the fundamental truth that all beings are created equal and deserve equal rights and protection under the law. This truth along with great compassion is my only motivation.

*Ultimate abolitionism* begins with *a clear understanding of spirit*, with seeing the dreamlike nature of reality and moving between the worlds of ultimate and conventional realities. The mystics, shamans, sages, magicians, buddhas, saints, prophets, and bodhisattvas can show us this way. This is the level where great spirits like Harriet reside and over time, we will learn how to navigate on this level more and more. As we grow in our spiritual practices, our faith in a higher power will also grow, which allows us to tap into unseen forces and use them for the good of others.

Civil rights hero John Lewis once said, "Do not get lost in a sea of despair. Be hopeful, be optimistic. Our struggle is not the struggle of a day, a week, a month, or a year, it is the struggle of a lifetime. Never, ever be afraid to make some noise and get in good trouble, necessary trouble."

Harriet says, *"I have great faith in this new generation, and I believe there is something very special moving through them. I see wisdom and great courage. For the benefit of all beings, please pick up the mantle and continue walking in the footsteps of your bravest ancestors. With faith in them and trust in our own hearts, we will find the strength to move big mountains and the power to part the seas. We can build a new movement together, united in our shared dream of a just world for all beings. Together, united in allyship, we can bring forth the dream that so many others have envisioned and worked so hard for. There is more work to do, and we need you. The Underground Allies will forever be on your side."*

## A Prayer

We give thanks to all the brave allies who supported
Harriet and the Underground, and we give thanks
to the new generation of abolitionists: William Still,
Frederick Douglass, Levi Coffin, Lucretia Coffin Mott,
John Brown, Thomas Garrett, Ellen Wright Garrison,
Elizabeth Cady Stanton, Diane Nash, Susan B. Anthony,
Sojourner Truth, Daniel Gibbons, Abigail Goodwin,
John Lewis, Stacey Abrams, Calvin Fairbank, Fannie Lou
Hamer, Charles Torrey, Maya Angelou, Ida B. Wells, Isaac
Hopper, Elijah Anderson, Thaddeus Stevens, Rev. John
Rankin, John Fairfield, David Ruggles, Nelson Mandela,
Martin Luther King Jr., Angela Davis, James Baldwin,
Colin Kaepernick, and the thousands of others who
helped our ancestors along their journeys to freedom.

# Chapter 11

IIIIIIIIIIIIIIIIIIIIIIIIIIIIIIII

# THE HEART
# OF WOMEN

Today, as I begin this chapter, it's International Women's Day, March 8, 2022. My assistant, who is in Mexico City, called to tell me. She's off to join a huge women's march there. "How perfect!" I say. As I head back to the cabin where I'm on a writing retreat, getting ready to start a session with Harriet, I wonder what Harriet will share today. I think we're going to talk about women. I know she is passionate about the rights and dignity of women.

Suddenly, I feel Harriet's spirit really close to me. I prepare myself to surrender and go on another journey with her, but instead, we just sit together quietly. I feel her come closer and closer until her spirit merges right into me and she enters into my heart. Our breathing becomes synchronized in the most beautiful way. I'm not shaking, dizzy, or overwhelmed by her powerful energy. We are, at last, in harmony, in sync and attuned, and it's magical. After a few minutes, I begin thinking about women and I sense Harriet is as well.

As we sit quietly with our hearts merged, I begin feeling and experiencing a deep and tender part of Harriet, soft, loving, and almost aching with vulnerability. She begins to speak, *"Oh, Child, the women . . ."* almost in a whisper and then stops, over and over, as we breathe in and out together. I feel it too, a deep concern for the feminine spirit. Half the world are women, and way too many are oppressed, beaten down, and denied their God-given right to be free. As we continue breathing together, Harriet begins chanting. It's a prayer: *"Heavenly Father, forgive them. Forgive them, for they know not what they do."*

As Harriet prays, I slowly begin seeing images of her sisters and understand her prayers. Three of her sisters were sold away from the family and it saddened Harriet throughout her life. The first, Mariah Ross, was sold when Harriet was a baby, and although Harriet was so young, she was aware of the deep grief her parents experienced at the loss of their daughter. Later, when Harriet was in her 20s, two other sisters, Linah Ross and Soph Ross, were taken away together and sold. It was a traumatic day she would never forget.

Harriet says, *"Child, I will always remember the sounds of the jingle-jangle of the horse-drawn wagons approaching in the distance, the noise of men shouting harshly and chains banging on wood. In that moment, my worst fears were coming to pass; the slave traders had arrived. Men who chose a life of slave trading were some of the cruelest human beings I ever knew. They were heartless, the lowest of the low, and their contorted smirks and merciless grins were twisted in delight while inflicting pain and suffering on Black men, women, and children. Child, there was a moment of calm in me, followed by an explosion of raw emotion when I heard my sisters scream for help. Their sorrowful cries echoed throughout the plantation and our whole family raced to the scene.*

*"I watched my beloved sisters Linah and Soph get handcuffed and forcibly dragged away. Linah called out to her young children and it damn near broke my heart. Her tiny daughter,*

Kessiah, stood weeping as she watched her mama violently
thrown onto the back of the wagon. I stood there watching
helplessly while our whole family begged and pleaded for their
release. What could we do? The men had whips and guns, the
law was on their side, and the owners who had agreed to it all
were nonchalantly watching from the veranda.

"They were probably taken far South to a cotton farm,
where they would grow and pick cotton morning, noon, and
night. They disappeared from our lives, and we never saw them
again. I have always believed women should be free and what
happened to my sisters was just not right, Child. Linah and
Soph were so kindhearted, intelligent, and thoughtful. Our
whole family cherished them, Child, we really did."

It feels touching and important to pay homage to Harriet's sisters. What happened to these young women encapsulates the experience of so many Black women during the years of slavery and even the century that followed.

Harriet and I continue sitting together, praying, and just breathing, and Harriet says, "Child, I never forgot about my sisters, and every mission, every task I completed, I honored them in some way. With every step I took, they were always with me deep in my heart." I feel as if I'm holding space for Harriet's deep loss. Praying with her feels like a sacred duty.

As we sit together, we begin chatting about the women we've loved and those who have departed this world. We're like two old storytellers smoking pipes and sharing our stories. Harriet says, "Child, I told you one of my stories; now you tell me one of yours." I pause for a few breaths as I think about my father's mother, Ms. Anna Mae French, and I say okay.

If you were to look up "strong, kindhearted Southern Black grandmother" in the encyclopedia or Wikipedia or a dictionary, you would almost certainly find a photo of my grandmother Anna Mae French. She was classic. She had a thick Black Southern accent, she was big and jolly, a devout Christian who loved everyone unconditionally. She loved to cook soul food dinners, especially huge ones on Sundays after church. She loved to talk, laugh, and tell funny stories about the past for hours and hours on end.

She told me that when she was a young woman at the small "Colored Only" movie theater in town watching *Gone with the Wind*, her water broke. She was nine months pregnant and so excited and absorbed in the movie, she didn't realize she was in full-blown labor until the last line of the film. Shortly after Scarlett O'Hara's final scene, my father was born.

Anna Mae never smoked, drank, or cursed. She had a deep sense of peace and forgiveness that she attributed directly to Jesus, and she would thank him out loud for it many times a day. She was incredibly generous despite having very little. She would never tell a lie and wouldn't take anyone's money if she felt it had been acquired through ill-gotten means. She was the keeper of the family history and had dozens of photo albums stacked to the ceiling and stuffed into every closet. She also had framed family photos covering every wall of her tiny home. While sitting on her living room couch when I visited her many years later, I saw a sea of smiling Black faces everywhere I looked. Grandma had a heart of gold, and she loved it when I visited. The moment I arrived, she would squeal, "My beautiful California granddaughter is here!" She'd then envelop me in her arms, bring me a giant cup of sweet iced tea, and stuff me with slice after slice of her famous lemon pound cake.

Anna Mae's mother was just 13 years old when Anna Mae was born. She never knew who her father was, and due to her mother's young age, she lived for many years with different foster parents. As a teenager, she met my grandfather and they moved to Wilmington, Delaware, into a tiny two-bedroom house, where she lived most of her life. Even today Wilmington is largely segregated, and she always lived in the Black side of town. She had seven children. My father was the second oldest, and the youngest, my uncle Wayne, had Down syndrome. She raised her seven children pretty much alone, because my grandfather was in the navy and was gone for months at a time aboard ships. And when he was at home, he drank, partied, had many girlfriends, and gambled their money away. He was a terrible husband, so she eventually divorced him and married another man whom she adored, but then he got sick and died.

She was always poor and had to accept the only job that was available for Black women of her era, which was to be a maid, cook, and nanny for white families in the rich part of town. Grandma Anna Mae spent her whole life in a maid's uniform, cooking, cleaning, and taking care of other people's children. She told me once that she helped raise many white children and it made her sad because she was never at home to raise her own seven children. She worked hard, often seven days a week and holidays, for little money, and she received little gratitude.

Grandma lived for many years under the oppressive system of Jim Crow and shared heartbreaking stories about all the racism she experienced. One time just after they moved to Delaware, she saved up her money and took a vacation to Atlantic City, just a couple of hours from Delaware. She'd always dreamed about swimming in the ocean. She was maybe 18, and someone snapped this amazing black-and-white photo of her posing modestly while standing on the beach in her one-piece bathing suit. She had a huge smile on her face. While she and I were sitting in her living room looking at this photo, she described how they were only allowed on a tiny strip of beach. It was against the law for her to walk on any other part of the beach. Signs saying, "Whites Only" were everywhere. I looked up at her while she was sharing that memory, and she just sighed loudly and said, "Oh well," then added, "Honey, we had so much fun on our little side of the beach that day!" and she burst out laughing. She had a genuine sense of equanimity about her life. She passed away a few years ago.

I say to Harriet, "They don't make women like that anymore. She was strong as hell and was so kind and cheerful. I'm sure she's in heaven smiling right now."

Harriet says, *"Yes, Child. She was resilient and underestimated, like so many women are. I see your grandmother's spirit in you, Child."*

I laugh doubtfully and say, "I don't think I could have dealt with one percent of what she went through."

Harriet says, *"Child, trust the light inside of you. Trust in your own good heart. You have so much power, you just don't realize it yet. You don't see yourself for who you truly are. You don't believe that the universe is on your side."*

Something in each of us longs for wholeness. Our hearts know when the scales of wisdom, justice, and truth are in or out of balance. We need the voices and stories of women, wise women, now more than ever. Women's spiritual teachings and especially women's stories of liberation have been left out of the texts of almost all the world's religions, and we're left feeling second-rate, which is a distorted view of reality. There are stories you haven't heard, especially stories of Black, brown, and indigenous women, that when told will be healing balm on our open wounds. The lives of our mothers, grandmothers, and sisters hold profound meaning, and their long-forgotten voices must now rise together.

So many people believe religion, spirituality, and enlightenment are reserved just for male priests, scholars, clergy, and monks. In many religions, women are still barred from holding power. We are considered unclean, even unsanitary, and are often belittled and put down. Most histories—not just religious—are recorded by colonizers and conquerors to suit their own purposes and views. Then they're passed down by males, mostly white and often misogynistic. Too many men, even today, hold deep prejudices toward women and the feminine. I always wonder where this deep mistrust, even hatred, of women began.

Harriet says, *"Child, the big problem lies in our creation stories, especially in the Western world. The dominant creation myth begins with Adam and Eve being thrown out of the garden, and it's Eve's fault. They get cut off from God. Child, if we keep on believing that our pain and misery is the fault of a woman, we'll continue creating a world that's full of torment and confusion."*

Our current blame-the-woman creation story has had a devasting impact not only on the hearts and minds of women but on humankind and Mother Earth herself. The folklore and stories we pass down generation after generation are important, they shape our views about who we are and where we come from. Women have lived feeling inferior for so long it's become woven deep into our DNA. Our mythology needs a big overhaul; it's a huge prison of the mind and it feels dangerous to keep believing in it. When it's believed and passed on, our negative ideas about the feminine take people in the opposite direction of love and compassion.

Harriet says, *"Religions should never be used as tools for hatred, control, and oppression of women. We must all start taking responsibility for our own hearts and minds. If we feel lost and separate from God and the Garden of Eden, it's no one's else's fault. It's too late for blaming. Now is the time to find our way home, to go back to the Promised Land. God loves everyone and there's nothin' you can do to change that. It doesn't matter what folks call God, this bright love shines on everything, all the time, and we're never separate from it."*

Since antiquity, women have been oppressed and even burned at the stake when they've spoken of their own divine relationships with God. Many died trying to share what they knew to be true. The good news is that every day, the forgotten, lost, and overlooked stories of heroic women are being found, stories of bravery, stories of wisdom, and stories of their spiritual insights. These stories, these wise women, are at last rising. And this includes Harriet Tubman's spiritual messages and teachings. The Gospel of Mary Magdalene was discovered in the late 19th century and is finally emerging as another feminist truth. The man who became the Buddha was supported every step of the way by his stepmother, his wife, and a young village girl named Sujata who saved his life at his moment of need, and at last, their stories are getting their due.

I have always felt a connection with Sujata, an important part of the story of Siddhartha Gautama's epic journey to enlightenment. The Buddha-to-be spent six long years in the forest practicing very strict meditation and renunciation. For long periods of time, according to the myth, he ate only a grain of rice a day. He never bathed, and his hair became long and matted, his body weak and emaciated, almost literally just a bag of bones. He was dying and the whole spirit world became deeply concerned.

One day he tried to stand up to go to the bathroom and he fell on his face. At that moment, a young girl who had spent all morning making a delicious bowl of rice pudding was walking through the forest on her way to offer it at a nearby temple. This was Sujata. When she saw the mangled man lying in the dirt, her heart filled with love and devotion, and she immediately offered the bowl of food to him. She helped him eat, then bathe in the river.

This story is symbolic of the feminine spirit. The Buddha-to-be was practicing in such a harsh way that he was unknowingly killing himself while trying to reach enlightenment. Sujata represents the divine feminine intervening to provide sustenance, balance, and nurturing. He realized he needed a middle-way approach, and Sujata helped show him the way.

I ask Harriet, "What if the women of the world, collectively, were to envision a new creation story, a new mythology about who we are and where we come from? I see an empowering new narrative, one we can pass down to our daughters and granddaughters!"

Harriet says, "*Yes, Child, something new must be born. Only birth can conquer death. It's time for the old narratives, the old programs, the old prisons to die. A new story must be written in the hearts of women, something new inscribed within our bodies and souls, and within the body of the earth itself. You and all the strong, living women today must break through, rejuvenate, and restore our creation story.*

"*It's a new day, Child, and I see women coming into great power, but many women and men are blind to it. I'm not talking about power over others. I'm talking real power, the ability to fulfill your purpose and complete your soul's task, Child, the ability to effect real change. If we want things to change, we can't just keep waitin' around. We need to believe in ourselves, and we need to make it happen."*

As Harriet and I continue chatting and telling stories, her softness remains. She begins to share more personal details about her life after the Civil War ended. Harriet says, *"Child, after the war was finally over and I took off my military uniform, I wanted to feel like a woman again. I wanted a soft bed, a comfortable home, a good husband, clean clothes, and some children. It was a different side of me, Child; it was more of my feminine side, and I liked it."*

In 1859, Harriet had acquired a piece of land in Auburn, New York, and this is where she would build her new life. A year before the war started, abolitionists Frances and William Seward had offered Harriet the opportunity to become a homeowner. It was a seven-acre farm, and they decided to offer it to Harriet for the price of $1,200. It had a wooden home, a barn, and a few other buildings on the property. They offered her a payment plan and she happily accepted. She took in boarders to make ends meet.

Her entire family came to join her, and before long a new love would enter her life. Harriet's first husband was John Tubman, and they were married for five years while she was still enslaved on the plantation in Maryland. He never believed in her and he refused to go with her to Philadelphia when she escaped even though he was a free man. He ended up leaving Harriet for another woman shortly after she went north. Harriet loved him very much and although she was heartbroken when he married another woman, for reasons unknown she decided to keep his last name.

Shortly after getting settled in her new home, Harriet fell in love with Private Nelson Charles, a young and handsome Black veteran whom she met during the war. He was honorably discharged and one day he magically appeared at her front door in search of housing. He was more than 20 years younger than she, and he had tuberculosis and many injuries from the war. Harriet was unconcerned about all of that, and she began to take care of him. They were officially married in Auburn Presbyterian Church at a large wedding in 1869. Harriet was never able to have children, so five years later they adopted a baby girl name Gertie.

Harriet says, *"Child, this was one of the happiest times in my life. It was such a hopeful time, and so many things had been accomplished. Slavery was over and I was no longer a fugitive. Charles and I started a big farm together with chickens, ducks, pigs. We grew fruits and vegetables and sold butter. My entire family was finally all together on a beautiful piece of land that I owned! It was time to take a much-needed break and enjoy family, friends, and my new husband. I rested for a few years, then I began to realize how terribly oppressed women were. We couldn't even vote, and this bothered me greatly."*

Harriet did take a much-needed break after the Civil War ended, but when her old Underground allies Susan B. Anthony and Elizabeth Cady Stanton called, she sprang into action. Harriet was called back into the world to be of service again. She was a revolutionist and believed in the equality of all people, Black and white, male and female. Many of Harriet's most devoted friends and supporters during her Underground Railroad years were now involved in the women's suffrage movement, and she began meeting regularly with Susan B. Anthony and many others who had a deep passion for women's freedom.

Harriet would try to change the world again by joining the woman's suffrage movement. The narrative of the hero's journey depicted in all the great myths fits Harriet *to a T*: the hero or heroine gives their life to something bigger than themselves. The 13th Amendment was finally passed, and the institution of slavery was finally abolished, so her next mission was working toward amending the Constitution to include women's right to vote. She spent many years on the road speaking out on the rights of women. She toured New York, Boston, and Washington giving speeches about all her experiences as a slave, as Moses the Liberator, and as a woman war general. It was during this time that two biographies of Harriet were written by Sarah H. Bradford. The first, *Scenes from the Life of Harriet Tubman*, was published in 1869, and the second, *Harriet, the Moses of Her People*, in 1886. Harriet never learned to read or write, but her speeches were captivating, and she was a very popular and sought-after speaker. She spent the remaining years of her life fighting for women's rights, especially those of Black women.

Harriet says, *"Child, it was dangerous work! We were always being attacked and mobs of enraged men showed up at every stop of our speaking tours. Most people don't realize how much we went through. We had to fight hard, and many women were jailed and persecuted and suffered physical abuse. In my visions I always saw the future. I saw a time when American women both Black and white would finally be free. I always saw that things were changing."*

Just six years after Harriet died, the 19th Amendment, which gave women full voting rights, was passed. Sitting quietly this evening with Harriet, my heart is so full of wonder at her incredible life. Harriet says, *"Child, I chose to 'come down' as a woman. I needed to show other women,* especially Black women, what they are capable of. Women must believe in themselves. We are capable of so much more than even we know. The women can save this world if only we believe we can. In fact, we must believe we can in order to do it."

Harriet says, "*Yes, Child, the universe and all of space, including the stars, the planets, the galaxies, and all other life-forms, are monitoring the tracks down here. People are crying out for help, and the earth itself is crying out for help. Others and I are trying hard to fix the tracks, and we're calling on every woman to help. Our work now is based on feminine wisdom, compassion, and lasting freedom. I encourage all womankind to unite in compassion so we can awaken faster. The ancestors, angels, and all the bodhisattvas are in this with you. To all the women, mothers, and grandmothers, we must wake up now. Remember who you are.*"

I shake my head in deep understanding that yes, we must reclaim our power and our magic. We're not just fighting for the soul of a nation, but also for the heart of this beautiful planet.

---

## A Prayer

We give thanks to every brave woman
throughout history who stood up for what is right.
We give thanks to the suffragettes and the
thousands of brave women who fought for freedom.
We send love and compassion to help heal the
feminine spirit on this planet. We send love to
Harriet's sisters and to all our sisters.

---

Harriet Tubman, circa 1887.
Photograph courtesy of the Ohio History Connection.

# Chapter 12

▒▒▒▒▒▒▒▒▒▒▒▒▒▒▒▒▒▒▒▒▒

# ON TO ZION
# WE GO

*"My life has always been a journey,"* Harriet tells me, *"a long ride with so many stops. But I never stop for too long, I must keep moving and so do you. You see, Child, we are all just travelers and passengers. We always have somewhere to go and something new to experience. Some stops are so beautiful that it can be so hard to leave, even when it's time. Other stops may be more painful than we can bear. Even dying is just another stop, a resting place till you're ready to get back on the train again. Life has so much goodness and so much pain; it's all a part of it."*

As I write these words, tears are rolling down my cheeks. While writing this book, I have often felt overcome by self-doubt, and Harriet was always there to encourage me to begin again and keep going. So, I would. Some part of me died along the way, though, a part that needed to go so something new could be born. My biggest awakening was the conscious movement from my head to my heart. I learned to see things with new eyes, and I became increasingly aware of many things I was previously unconscious of. Growth is learning, discovering who we truly are.

I'm still in amazement with this journey, with this story, with this book, and with the spirit of Harriet Tubman. She is everything I could have imagined and so much more. She is real, she is alive, and I am eternally grateful for this experience. Why Harriet came to talk to me and share her heart remains a mystery. Maybe one day I'll understand, and perhaps it doesn't really matter. Regardless of why, I have been changed by the experience.

I hope that, in reading this book, you will find your own deep connection to Harriet, to her love, her strength, and her incredible wisdom. She is a teacher, a protector, and a devoted friend for all who need one. Her arms are wide open. She isn't just my ancestor; she's everyone's ancestor. Her spirit is awakening within me, and you, and this beautiful and broken world we all love so much. I feel a sense of accomplishment that I completed the task she gave me, and at the same time, I know it's not over. In fact, it's just beginning. I have already boarded the next train, and I'll spend the rest of my life talking about Ms. Harriet Tubman, reflecting on her legacy, and sharing her courageous story with others.

Harriet taught me that we're much more than we realize, that love is always there, that faith will move mountains, and that we're never alone. She taught me that one person can start a movement, but that it takes a committed community to sustain it. She taught me that compassion is the strongest force in the universe, that no matter how dark the sky is, the sun will always rise. She taught me to always stand up for what you believe in, that the spirit world is real, that goodness will always prevail in the end. With Harriet, I learned to surrender to a higher power, that it's okay to be underestimated as long as you know who you are, that God loves everyone unconditionally, that everything is alive, and everything has spirit. In spending hours and hours with Harriet Tubman, I learned the power of prayer, that all chains can be broken, that our ancestors hear us, and that if we're given a task, we can complete it. I learned that the Promised Land is real and that it's inside each of us, that we have great power, that our true nature is light, and to never give up on ourselves. Through it all I know now that magic exists, we can always find a way, that courage is a great virtue and divine patience is always necessary. And finally, I learned that the Underground Railroad is real and so is Zion.

Harriet says, "*Yes, Child, yes! You have been through a process called 'conduction.' It means delivered, transported, carried—it's a form of transmission. Now you will go on to help others find the higher path, the ancient pathway that's been buried and forgotten until it's rediscovered. Child, clear back the branches, move aside the stones that are covering the path, and put up new signs pointing everyone in the direction of freedom. That's what all good teachers and conductors do: they help others see what has been there all along.*

"*We have entered a new time and a new level, Child. I'm helping you, but you're also helping me. We conducted this book together. The spirit world and the ancestors always need strong helpers, and they call on certain folks from time to time to help them complete different tasks.*

"*It's good you said yes, Child, and in the future always try to say yes.*"

Harriet Tubman was a visionary, a prophet who saw the future. She believed—she *knew*—that every child born has a God-given right to be free. She knew that women, children, and people of color all have an equal right to live in peace. She saw a just world where everyone has access to food, shelter, education, and health care, the kind of country so many of us dream of. We must keep the truth alive that all beings are created equal.

I believe deep down we all know that every human being is the same. We have different cultures, languages, religions, skin colors, genders, sexual orientations, and personalities, but we are fundamentally the same. Our bodies share 99.9 percent of the same DNA, and the same chemistry and elemental components. We share the same struggles and aspirations. We all long for happiness and meaning in a world filled with uncertainty. We all experience joy and pain while grappling with the mysteries of birth, aging, and death. As Dr. King said so beautifully, "We are caught in an inescapable network of mutuality, tied in a single garment of destiny. Whatever affects one directly, affects all indirectly." As Underground allies, we must remember that all of humanity is cut from the same cloth and is born from the same bright and wondrous source.

What makes us different from one another is our level of wisdom, which has nothing to do with skin tone, gender, or our physical body at all. A wise being understands this and has learned that seeds planted in hatred and anger lead to pain and suffering and seeds planted in love and compassion lead to happiness. Everything is so complex yet so simple, my friends. Love is all there is.

When holding seeds of wisdom in one hand and seeds of delusion in the other, a wise being will skillfully discern between the two. Wisdom sees through the delusion. It knows that all humanity is an interconnected web of life and that everyone and everything belongs to it. Our beautiful and wise hearts will *always* choose to plant the wise seed, because our hearts know that I am "you" and "you" are me and that we *inter-are*. This is what drove the Buddha to sit under the Bodhi tree and Moses to climb Mount Sinai. It's what awakened Harriet's heart and opened the Underground Railroad. It is our innate desire to plant the seed of wisdom for ourselves and for humanity. The prisons in our minds will always plant seeds of delusion and lies—until we finally *wake up.*

Systems theory shows us that right before a system collapses, there is often chaos and confusion. If we look at our global situation from this perspective, we'll see not merely that there is aggression and disorder, but that the old order is falling apart. We're a system in collapse no matter how hard some people fight to sustain it and prop it back up. Our survival is predicated on the evolution of consciousness based on the principles of universal sisterhood and brotherhood. The spirits of the Underground movement are rising again to help us get through the big storms that are brewing on the horizon.

We stand together to meet the challenges as they are arising *again.* This next stage takes courage as we learn to stand up for each other, to face our fears by doing the things that scare us. We have to encounter what we don't want to face. You have enormous power and it's important to consider how to use it. It doesn't matter if you're in a wheelchair, elderly, or young. Neither does your ethnicity, sexual orientation, or gender. What's important is believing that we have some power, and it's rising in so many of us. Whether our faith comes from God, Jesus, Buddha, Krishna, Mohammad, the universe, the earth, or Harriet Tubman, ultimately trust and confidence will move us to higher ground, where we become lamps in the darkness by our resiliency and our willingness to stay the course. This is who we are. We embody this. Please, friends, don't go back to sleep.

‖‖‖‖‖‖‖

Our great ancestor Harriet Tubman died at the age of 91 of pneumonia, surrounded by her close friends and family. It was March 10, 1913, and she was buried with full military honors at Fort Hill Cemetery in Auburn, New York. Her last words were from the Bible: "I go and prepare a place for you." Then she closed her eyes. And just like that her spirit was set free again. I always imagine an army of angels coming to meet her and each holding her with such tenderness.

As I wrote this last chapter, imagining Harriet lying surrounded by angels, I saw one final powerful vision that I will always remember because it brought so much comfort to me.

Not only was she held in the arms of angels, but in her own arms she was holding others: George Floyd, Ahmaud Arbery, Breonna Taylor, and so many more. I saw the four little girls who were murdered during their Bible study when the 16th Street Baptist Church in Birmingham, Alabama, was bombed on September 15, 1963. I saw Medgar Wiley Evers, the American civil-rights activist and the NAACP's first field secretary in Mississippi, who was assassinated by a white supremacist. They were all there— thousands of martyrs, freedom fighters, and great spirits— and Harriet held them all. She rescued them; she made a place for them. They were all in her arms, laughing and smiling. She wanted me to share this vision so we know that they are safe with her.

# ACKNOWLEDGMENTS

There are two very special people I would like to personally thank. I thank them because they believed in me when others didn't. They believed in me when it was hard to believe in myself. Without them, this book wouldn't be possible. I have infinite gratitude for my beloved teacher Jack Kornfield and for Patty Gift, the vice president of Hay House. I bow to you both a thousand times. Thank you for seeing me and for seeing the vision of what was possible long before I did.

# ABOUT THE AUTHOR

▪▪▪▪▪▪▪▪▪▪▪▪▪▪▪▪▪▪▪▪▪▪▪▪▪▪▪▪▪▪▪▪▪▪▪▪▪▪▪▪▪▪▪▪▪▪▪▪▪▪▪▪▪▪▪▪▪▪▪▪▪▪▪▪▪▪▪▪▪▪▪▪

Spring Washam is a well-known meditation teacher, author, and visionary leader based in Oakland, California. She is the author of *A Fierce Heart: Finding Strength, Courage, and Wisdom in Any Moment* and her newest book, *The Spirit of Harriet Tubman: Awakening from the Underground.*

Spring is considered a pioneer in bringing mindfulness-based healing practices to diverse communities. She is one of the founding teachers at the East Bay Meditation Center, located in downtown Oakland. She received extensive training by Jack Kornfield, is a member of the Teachers Council at Spirit Rock Meditation Center in Northern California, and has practiced and studied Buddhist philosophy in both the Theravada and Tibetan schools of Buddhism since 1999. In addition to being a teacher, she is also a shamanic practitioner and has studied indigenous healing practices since 2008. She is the founder of Lotus Vine Journeys, an organization that blends indigenous healing practices with Buddhist wisdom in South America. Her writing and teachings have appeared in many online journals and publications such as *Lion's Roar*, *Tricycle*, and *Belief.net*. She has been a guest on many popular podcasts and radio shows. She currently travels and teaches meditation retreats, workshops, and classes worldwide.

www.springwasham.com

# Hay House Titles of Related Interest

▓▓▓▓▓▓▓▓▓▓▓▓▓▓▓▓▓▓▓▓▓▓▓▓▓▓▓▓▓▓▓▓▓▓▓▓▓▓▓▓▓▓▓▓▓▓▓▓

*YOU CAN HEAL YOUR LIFE, the movie,*
starring Louise Hay & Friends
(available as an online streaming video)
www.hayhouse.com/louise-movie

*THE SHIFT, the movie,*
starring Dr. Wayne W. Dyer
(available as an online streaming video)
www.hayhouse.com/the-shift-movie

▓▓▓▓▓▓▓▓▓▓▓▓▓▓▓▓▓▓▓▓▓▓▓▓▓▓▓

*BLACK GIRL IN LOVE (WITH HERSELF): A Guide to Self-Love,*
*Healing, and Creating the Life You Truly Deserve,* by Trey Anthony

*THE DHARMA IN DIFFICULT TIMES: Finding Your Calling in*
*Times of Loss, Change, Struggle, and Doubt,* by Stephen Cope

*A FIERCE HEART: Finding Strength, Courage, and Wisdom*
*in Any Moment,* by Spring Washam

*KNOW JUSTICE KNOW PEACE: A Transformative Journey*
*of Social Justice, Anti-Racism, and Healing through the Power*
*of the Enneagram,* by Deborah Threadgill Egerton, Ph.D.

All of the above are available at your local bookstore,
or may be ordered by contacting Hay House (see next page).

▓▓▓▓▓▓▓▓▓▓▓▓▓▓▓▓▓▓▓▓▓▓▓▓▓▓▓

We hope you enjoyed this Hay House book. If you'd like to receive our online catalog featuring additional information on Hay House books and products, or if you'd like to find out more about the Hay Foundation, please contact:

Hay House, Inc., P.O. Box 5100, Carlsbad, CA 92018-5100
(760) 431-7695 or (800) 654-5126
(760) 431-6948 (fax) or (800) 650-5115 (fax)
www.hayhouse.com® • www.hayfoundation.org

———

*Published in Australia by:* Hay House Australia Pty. Ltd.,
18/36 Ralph St., Alexandria NSW 2015
*Phone:* 612-9669-4299 • *Fax:* 612-9669-4144
www.hayhouse.com.au

*Published in the United Kingdom by:* Hay House UK, Ltd.,
The Sixth Floor, Watson House, 54 Baker Street, London W1U 7BU
*Phone:* +44 (0)20 3927 7290 • *Fax:* +44 (0)20 3927 7291
www.hayhouse.co.uk

*Published in India by:* Hay House Publishers India,
Muskaan Complex, Plot No. 3, B-2, Vasant Kunj, New Delhi 110 070
*Phone:* 91-11-4176-1620 • *Fax:* 91-11-4176-1630
www.hayhouse.co.in

———

## Access New Knowledge.
## Anytime. Anywhere.

Learn and evolve at your own pace
with the world's leading experts.

www.hayhouseU.com